FIBER GLASS BOATS

Construction, Repair, and Maintenance

John Roberts

W·W·NORTON & COMPANY

NEW YORK   LONDON

3-88 BT 2200

Copyright © 1984 by John A. Roberts

ALL RIGHTS RESERVED

Published simultaneously in Canada by
Penguin Books Canada Ltd,
2801 John Street, Markham, Ontario L3R 1B4.

PRINTED IN THE UNITED STATES OF AMERICA

Library of Congress Cataloging in Publication Data

Roberts, John Arthur, 1938–
Fiber glass boats.

1. Fiber glass boats. I. Title.

VM321.R63 1984   623.8′207   83-8234

ISBN 0-393-03291-4

W. W. Norton & Company, Inc., 500 Fifth Avenue, New York, N. Y. 10110
W. W. Norton & Company Ltd., 37 Great Russell Street, London WC1B 3NU

3 4 5 6 7 8 9 0

Acknowledgments

This book would not have been written were it not for the encouragement, support, and help of many people. Among those individuals are Tony Gibbs, who, when he was editor of *Yachting,* suggested that I write this book and then led me to W. W. Norton's Eric Swenson, who fashioned my manuscript into the product you hold in your hands.

Between that beginning and end, there was a large research project in which bits and pieces were gleaned from sources ranging from an early book by the late Boughton S. Cobb, Jr., about fiber glass boat construction to contemporary articles in *Motorboating & Sailing, Sail,* and *Yachting* magazines to interviews of experts about the variety of materials used in boat construction to interviews with a number of boat builders and visits to their plants to telephone calls to whatever other sources the web of research led. All of that was then seasoned by what we've learned less formally during the past several years through our own experience in boating—including finishing out our Vancouver 36 sailboat *Sea Sparrow,* which we purchased as a "kit" boat—and in writing magazine articles about boats and boating.

Although the list of individuals who gave of their expertise and experience is long, there are four in particular whom I would mention: Stewart Anderson, marketing director for marine resins, and Earl Zion, a Composites Laboratory supervisor, both at Owens Corning Fiberglas Company; Robert Arthur, senior material and process engineer at Hatteras Yachts; and Earl Blackwell, director of engineering at Gulfstar, Inc. These four not only were helpful during my research activities, but also served as technical reviewers for the manuscript.

Others who provided information for the book and, in some

instances, helped provide specialized technical review included technical and marketing personnel from American Cyanamid Company (prepregs); American Klegecell, Inc. (Klegecell foam); Amoco Chemicals Corporation (supplier to resin manufacturers); Baltek Corporation (balsa core); boating entrepreneur Ian Bruce; Boat Life Industries (sealants/adhesives); the Cal Boats Division of Bangor Punta Marine; Du Pont Company (Kevlar reinforcing fabrics, Nomex honeycomb, resins); Force Engineering (Stiletto catamarans); Gougeon Brothers, Inc. (WEST System of cold-molded wood boat construction); Hidden Harbor Boat Works, Inc.; Islander Yachts; James Walker Manufacturing Co. (antislip deck covering); 3M Company (sealants/adhesives); Murray Chris-Craft Cruisers, Inc.; Orcon, Inc. (unidirectional fabrics of exotic fibers); Owens Corning Fiberglas Company (resins, reinforcing materials, construction methods, repairs, and maintenance); Proform, Inc. (triaxial reinforcing fabrics); Rule Industries (sealants/adhesives); Seeman Fiberglass, Inc. (C-flex); The American Bureau of Shipping; The Society of the Plastics Industry (technical papers); Tillotson-Pearson (carbon fiber spars); Torin, Inc. (Airex foam); USS Chemicals Co. (resins); Vanguard, Inc.; Viking Yachts; Wellcraft Marine; and West Point Pepperell (Coremat).

Even with the contributions from all of these and other sources, however, this book would not have been written without the encouragement, support, and constructive editorial assistance of my sailing partner and wife, Susan, and the understanding of our children, who saw their Mom and Dad working on "the book" when sometimes they might like to have had us spending that time with them.

John A. Roberts

Galena, Maryland
April 1983

Contents

can choose from a variety of core materials ranging from balsa to PVC foam to a paperlike honeycomb material. Each has its advantages and disadvantages. Some require different laminating techniques than others.

5 Custom Hulls

Three basic systems allow amateurs and professionals alike to use FRP technology for construction of custom hulls. One involves use of a foam core placed over a "male" mold, a framework built to the size and shape of the inside of the hull. Another involves use of a fiber glass "plank" that is stapled over a male mold. The third, the WEST system, involves laminating resin-saturated strips of wood over the mold. All three systems require a large amount of labor in fairing the outer surface of the hull to obtain a smooth finish.

6 Interior Components

Fiber glass boats rely upon interior components to reinforce the outer shell of the hull and deck. Approaches builders utilize range from the now traditional method of bonding all interior components to the hull and deck to use of complete hull liners to use of reinforcing grid systems of stringers and frames.

7 The Deck and Cabin House

The deck and cabin house are critical structural components of the overall boat. Solid FRP can be used, but usually composite construction is preferred because it provides needed strength with less weight. However, no matter how well done the deck may be, the overall outer shell will be only as strong as the joint between the hull and deck.

8 Marine Sealants

A wide range of marine sealants are available to modern boat builders, each characterized by its own advantages and disadvantages. Products range from traditional fish oil bedding compounds to silicone sealants to modern polysulfide and polyurethane adhesive / sealants.

9 The Finished Boat

Rapidly changing technology for FRP boat construction makes it more important than ever to have boats surveyed by a qualified marine surveyor before any purchase is completed. There is much an informed buyer can do, however, to help himself in narrowing the field to a choice of one or two boats. A detailed checklist helps amateurs in their search.

10 Maintenance

Despite rumors, FRP boats are not maintenance free. Regular waxing helps maintain gel coat appearance, and prompt repair of even minor scratches and dings helps protect the laminate from water. But in time, even a well-maintained gel coat will need renewing—preferably with one of the two-part polyurethane coatings now on the market.

11 Repairs with FRP

One advantage of FRP construction is the ease with which even serious damage can be repaired—if necessary, even by amateurs. Different steps may be involved, however, depending upon whether the laminate is a solid lay-up or cored, and whether a liner, stringers, or bulkheads are involved. While amateurs may want to effect small repairs, discretion suggests letting experts take on any major repairs, if there is any choice in the matter.

12 A Look Ahead

The quest for improved performance, the availability of new materials, and the application of computers to boat design, engineering, and stress testing are bringing boat building closer to a science. Computers also have a role to play in improving production line efficiency. Prepregs and injection molding may be the competing technologies of the late 1980s.

FIBER GLASS
BOATS

1

The Fiber Glass Evolution
A Continuing Process

No single development in modern times has had more impact on boating than the application of fiber glass technology to boat construction. Before fiber glass, pleasure boating was the domain of a relatively small number of people. Today pleasure boating in one form or another is enjoyed by nearly a third of our U.S. population. Wood, of course, was then the principal boat-building material for pleasure boats, as it had been for centuries. A few larger yachts were made of steel. Today pleasure boats made of wood are the exception; fiber glass is almost the rule. Boat building, once principally the province of local craftsmen and a small number of such old line companies as Chris Craft, Matthews, and Trumpy, now includes hundreds of companies. These range in size from small local yards turning out a few boats each year to such large international conglomerates as AMF, Inc., whose products extend from the ubiquitous Sunfish to the full line of Hatteras Yachts, which now includes a 65-foot motor sailer. Production methods vary from the traditional "one piece at a time" to high-volume production lines capable of turning out hundreds of boats each month in a variety of sizes and models, with annual color and detail changes to differentiate each model year, *à la* Detroit (Photo 1).

1. Evolution of fiber glass boat construction has enabled large-volume builders to adopt assembly line and model differentiation techniques reminiscent of Detroit's automakers. (Photo by Susan Roberts)

The changes have been particularly dramatic on the sailing side of the industry. Before 1959, there was no real sailboat industry. Sailboats were mainly small day sailers or class boats for racing. Larger boats for cruising or offshore racing were mostly custom built, even those built to traditional or local designs. Today there are still custom sailboats being built—mostly for offshore racing—but sailing as well as powerboating has entered the age of "production boats." Entire new markets have been developed, for example, the bareboat charter industry and one-design racing, with the result that thousands of sailboats ranging in size from about 10 to 70 feet or larger are coming out of U.S. production facilities each year.

The development of fiber glass technology for boat building

was not an easy birth process. A variety of companies, most of which did not survive the effort, worked through the late 1940s and the 1950s to bring together the materials, techniques, and public readiness needed to begin the fiber glass revolution in boating. In 1950, according to one report, only 22 boats made of fiber glass—mostly runabouts—were exhibited at boat shows. Two years later, the U.S. Coast Guard commissioned three 40-foot patrol boats made of fiber glass skins over aluminum framing. In the mid-1950s, Philip L. Rhodes became the first yacht designer to use fiber glass construction, but while his 40-foot Bounty II design, introduced in 1956, was a market success, it was to be the forerunner of the fiber glass revolution, not its beginning. Its production run was cut short by the builder's financial failure, leaving it to Pearson to launch the modern fiber glass sailboat industry in 1959 with its 28-foot Triton sloop.

That same year, Willis Slane, the founder of Hatteras Yacht Co., brought the powerboat industry to the brink of the same revolution by announcing his plans to build a fiber glass sport fishing boat. Although the industry had been creeping toward fiberglass for several years, its use was mostly limited to small boats, for example, the Boston Whaler, introduced in 1956. The big-boat market, however, remained stolidly wooden—until Slane. The story may be apocryphal, but the origin of Hatteras Yachts is said to be Slane's frustration with waiting several days before he and some friends could go fishing off Cape Hatteras because the ocean was too rough for the wood boat they planned to use. While waiting for the seas to abate, Slane and his companions decided to use "that newfangled fiber glass" to build a boat with which they could fish even in the rough waters off Cape Hatteras. The introduction a year later (1960) of the Hatteras 41 and, at about the same time, a fiber glass version of the Bertram 31, marked the beginning of the end of traditional wood construction in most of the boating industry. A year later, 1961, more than half of the boats at the New York Boat Show were made of fiber glass. Yet even after that, it took the rest of the 1960s for the industry to be weaned from the tradition of wood, and most of the 1970s for builders to stop apologizing for the change.

Today more change is afoot—change encouraged by the rising costs of materials and labor; by growing market demand for lighter, faster, more fuel-efficient boats; and, on the powerboat side, expectation among builders of smaller boats that they will have to adapt to smaller engines as Detroit cuts back on its production of V-8 engine blocks. In response to these pressures, industry leaders are looking beyond the basic fiber glass technology they have relied upon for the past 25 years to find improved ways of building their boats. As a result, engineers, composite construction, materials testing, computer-assisted design, structural analysis, new molding techniques, and even computerized production systems are becoming increasingly important to the pleasure boat industry.

Traditionally—if one can speak of tradition in a technology barely 25 years old—fiber glass construction techniques have involved a mixture of glass fibers and plastic resins. Comparison has often been made to reinforced concrete, in which a network of steel wire or rods is put in place, wood forms are erected as molds, and the concrete is poured into the forms to encase the steel latticework. The resulting structure is many times stronger than the sum of the two components.

A fiber glass hull or deck is, in effect, a first cousin to "reinforced concrete." The steel wire, however, has been replaced by glass fibers, usually held together in either a loose feltlike fabric or a coarse woven material. The rough wooden forms generally have been replaced by a highly polished mold, and the concrete has given way to some form of plastic resin. Obviously, the material should be called "reinforced plastic" rather than fiber glass, and it is in some countries. The fact that it is not in the United States is a tribute to the marketing efforts of the Owens-Corning Fiberglas Corporation on behalf of its Fiberglas trademark. Outside of the United States, one hears of "glass-reinforced plastic" (GRP) or "fiber-reinforced plastic" (FRP) to describe this method of construction. Limited efforts are now being made in the United States by producers of competitive reinforcing fibers to popularize the concept of fiber-reinforced plastic.

From a practical viewpoint, it makes little difference what this form of boat construction is called. It simply is no longer possible for a single word or phrase to tell a prospective boat buyer much about the construction of the boat he is considering, for the technology we call fiber glass construction for boats has been expanded to include a broad range of materials, some of which can replace all or part of the glass in traditional fiber glass construction. Some of these materials have been used to a limited extent in the industry for a number of years but are now finding more widespread use; others have been used to good advantage in the aerospace industry but are new to boating; and one, the WEST system of cold-molded wood construction, represents a marriage of the tradition of wood with modern plastic resins and reinforcing fibers.

The first step most builders are taking (or have taken) toward more advanced technology is the use of so-called "core" materials to form a composite or "sandwich" construction. In this construction method, the inner and outer layers of fiber glass material are analogous to two slices of bread in a "sandwich" and the core represents the piece of cheese in the middle.

The function of the core is to increase the stiffness and, ultimately, the overall strength of the hull or deck. The principle involved is that of an I beam, in which two horizontal layers of steel are held apart by a vertical section (Fig. 1a). If one walks on an I beam, it will not bend, because both the top and bottom horizontal layers must bend together, and they cannot. The fact that the two layers are held a fixed distance apart means that the bottom layer must stretch (or tear) (Fig. 1b) to accommodate any downward bend in the top layer because it has farther to travel. (It's like being in the outside lane when driving around a curve; your car has to travel farther than the car in the inside lane.) The core material in fiber glass composite construction serves the same function as the vertical member of the I beam, increasing stiffness by holding the two outer layers a distance apart from one another (Fig. 2), letting engineers use the mechanical properties of the fiber glass laminate to better advantage.

There are at least seven core materials being used by the boating industry today. Each of these materials has advantages and disadvantages. Some are suitable for use in both hulls and decks; the remainder have more limited application. Balsa and plywood, for example, have been used to some extent by pro-

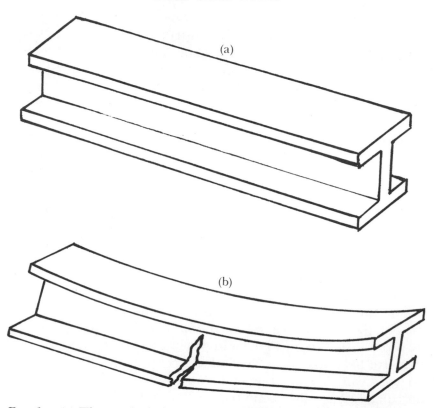

FIG. 1. (a) The vertical piece in the steel I beam holds two horizontal pieces a fixed distance apart. It is the horizontal "skins" that bear the major loads. (b) If too much weight is applied to the steel I beam from the top, the bottom piece must either stretch or tear for the beam to bend significantly. The same principal applies to cored fiber glass laminates.

duction boat builders for a number of years: plywood principally to strengthen decks and transoms, and balsa to stiffen hulls and decks. Today use of balsa core is increasing significantly. Other core materials, such as rigid polyvinyl chloride (PVC) foams (e.g., Klegecell) and semirigid PVC foams (e.g., Airex) have been used in custom boat construction for many years, but they too are now finding wider use in production boats. Two other core materials are sold under the trademarks Coremat and Nomex honeycomb, but they are much less commonly used.

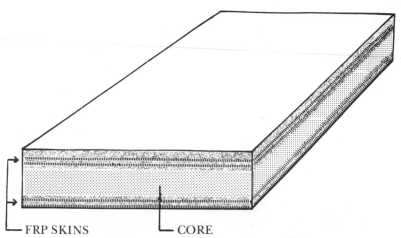

FRP SKINS ⌐ CORE

FIG. 2. In an FRP composite, the outer and inner skins are separated by a "core" material, most often plywood, balsa, or PVC foam. The core serves the same function as the vertical piece in the steel I beam.

Polyurethane foam also is used by some builders as a coring material, but its use is limited.

Some builders also are beginning to use different reinforcing systems. For example, a few builders are shifting away from woven fiber glass materials to fabrics in which nearly all of the glass fibers run in a single direction. This is the so-called "unidirectional" roving we read about in boating magazines. Another development is the use of two or three thicknesses of unidirectional roving made into a single fabric, but with the fibers in each layer oriented in different directions. Other developments include the use of a high-strength fiber glass material known as S-glass, of Kevlar aramid fibers, and of carbon fibers. All three of these materials have been widely used by the aerospace industry, where the importance of weight savings has outweighed costs. The same consideration—the desire to save weight—is now leading to increased use of these materials in the boating industry as well. The Kevlar and carbon fibers, of course, are not "fiber glass" materials; they are instead organic fibers.

Looking ahead, we can see the beginnings of still other technology in today's boating industry. The use of reinforcing fabrics impregnated with resin at a chemical plant and then shipped to the boat plant will offer some builders a major advantage in quality control in their fiber glass lay-ups. Vacuum molding is an old technique but has not been used much in the industry except in custom construction. However, the growing interest in preimpregnated reinforcing fabrics—called "prepregs"—and the efforts to adapt high-volume injection molding technology to boat construction suggest that vacuum-assisted molding techniques in one form or another will probably find a significant place in production boat building as we move further into the 1980s.

Similarly, the trend toward the use of more complex construction systems and the expanded use of aerospace materials is forcing the industry to place greater emphasis on materials testing and design engineering. The availability of improved computer technology and the need to make more efficient use of people and materials is leading to use of computers for boat design, production of engineering drawings, and, possibly, operation of some segments of the production line. All of these developments are affecting boat construction; most of these developments are discussed in the chapters ahead.

2

Resins and Reinforcement
Fundamental but Increasingly Complex

Builders have a variety of options when they construct a fiber glass boat. They begin with choice of gel coat resin, laminating resins, and reinforcing materials—the latter usually conventional fiber glass fabrics, but possibly one or more of the so-called "exotic" materials used in the aerospace industry. The choices the builders make can have important impact on the finished boat.

RESINS

Plastic resins take a variety of forms, but those used in the marine industry normally are shipped to the boat builder as a syrupy liquid. Large builders purchase these resins by the tank truck; smaller builders may buy their resin in 55-gallon drums; you and I will most often buy our resin packaged in containers of 5 gallons or less.

Although there may be important differences from one resin to another, all share one common characteristic: They consist of a mixture of short chemical chains called polymers. These polymer chains (picture them as short sections of anchor chain) are sitting in the can waiting to be hooked up together from every direction in a process called "cross-linking." As the resin cures, a chemical reaction takes place that forms "links" between the polymers. These links tie the chains from all directions until, when the cure is complete, they are locked into place in the hardened plastic. If there is an excess of cross-linking, the plastic may become so hard as to be brittle; if there is a shortage of cross-linking, it may be less tough or softer than desired.

In general, resins can be grouped according to their function. One group includes gel coat resins; the other includes laminating resins.

The gel coat of a boat is the hard, smooth outer surface of plastic that must, unless it is painted, withstand continuous exposure to the elements as well as whatever other abuse the boat's surface receives. Laminating resins, on the other hand, are used to encapsulate the reinforcing fibers and bond each successive layer (lamination) of reinforcing fabric to the layer before it. Harking back to the comparison with reinforced concrete, the gel coat is analogous to the plaster coating often used to give a finished look to the outer surface of a concrete structure. The laminating resin, on the other hand, is analogous to the concrete itself.

Three basic kinds of resin are used in the marine industry today. By far the most common are unsaturated polyester resins. A long way behind them in popularity are the epoxies, and back still farther in the running are the newer vinylester resins.

Within each of these basic categories, there may be important differences from resin to resin. When we realize, however, that in some ways making a plastic resin is similar to making a good soup, the variation from resin to resin is easily understood. In the kitchen, the cook begins with the basic ingredients for his soup and then adds a variety of lesser ingredients and spices to obtain the consistency and flavor he wants. Sometimes, he may even vary one of the basic ingredients.

In the chemical laboratory, a resin manufacturer follows a similar path. He begins with basic ingredients and then experiments until he finds the combination needed to provide the characteristics he wants in the resin. Some resins are formu-

lated to resist sagging or running. Some are formulated to minimize shrinkage as they cure to reduce fiber print-through from
the reinforcing fabric. Others are formulated to provide flame-
retardent properties. And still others may combine these and
other characteristics. The point is that boat builders can choose
from a variety of different resins.

Polyester Resins

About 80 to 90 percent of the resins used in marine fiber
glass construction today are polyester resins, including virtually
all gel coat resins. While there is a variety of recipes for polyester resins, all generally include five basic elements.

An "unsaturated" acid, usually maleic acid. The amount of
maleic (mah-LAY-ick) acid controls the amount of cross-linking
that will take place. Maleic acid represents from 25 to 40 percent of the acid content of standard general-purpose laminating resins used in the boating industry. The closer the maleic
acid content is to 40 percent, the tougher, more corrosion resistant the resin will be. As is often the case, however, there can
be too much of a good thing; in this instance, too much maleic
acid may result in excessive cross-linking, yielding a brittle resin.

A "saturated" acid, usually orthophthalic (ortho-THAL-lick)
acid, but sometimes blended with or replaced by isophthalic (iso-
THAL-lick) acid. The choice of saturated acids can affect the
water resistance, chemical resistance, and toughness of the cured
resin, as well as its cost. The "saturated" acid makes up the
remaining 60 to 75 percent of the acid content of standard laminating resins for the marine industry.

An alcohol, usually propylene glycol, which provides good
water resistance. However, most resin producers add some
diethylene glycol to provide increased resilience to the cured
resin and to reduce costs. A third glycol, neopentyl glycol, is
sometimes substituted for all or part of the other glycols to
improve performance in gel coat resins. The choice and blend
of alcohols will affect both the finished properties and cost of
the resin.

A monomer, generally styrene. The styrene has a dual function: (1) It acts as a solvent and (2) it serves as an active participant in the chemical reaction by which the resin cures. Without the styrene, the resin would be a hard solid consisting of many polymer chains. These chains are dissolved in the styrene so that the resin will flow. When the curing reaction begins, however, the styrene reacts with the polymers to form the cross-links that tie the chains together. In theory, all of the styrene stays in the resin to form cross-links; in practice, some styrene evaporates. Because styrene is highly flammable, its use presents an obvious fire hazard against which builders must guard themselves. In addition, there is concern about possible health effects upon employees from long-term exposure to high levels of styrene in the workplace. As a result, resin producers are developing styrene-suppressed resins that use an additive designed to rise quickly to the surface of the resin to form a barrier preventing evaporation of styrene.

An inhibitor, a chemical used to prevent the styrene from reacting with the polymer chains prematurely.

In general, typical marine resins are of similar composition. However, resin performance is affected by changes in glycols and the mixture of acids chosen by the resin producer. However, resin performance also can be affected—often in a negative manner—by use of fillers and extenders at the boat factory to stretch the mileage from each gallon of resin or to make the resin easier to work with. Usually boat builders are better advised to select a resin already formulated to provide the desired coverage and application characteristics than to modify the resin in their own shops.

Polyester resins also are characterized by their curing system. All that is generally needed to start the curing reaction is a small amount (a few teaspoons per gallon) of the initiator catalyst, typically the chemical methyl ethyl ketone (MEK) peroxide. Once started, the reaction proceeds on its own; most often, all of the necessary ingredients are contained within the resin itself.

After the MEK initiator has been added, the resin retains its liquid character for a period of time—typically 20 to 40 minutes—then rather suddenly enters a phase called "gelation." In other words, the resin becomes jellylike as the styrene forms the cross-links between polymer chains. Gelation is the most critical part of the curing process. After gelling has begun, the resin should not be disturbed lest irreversible damage be done. Once started, the cure is driven by heat released by the curing process itself. Depending upon the resin used and the thickness of the resin layer, the heat released by this polymerization reaction may be very great, typically between 300 and 400°F in a 100-gram mass of resin that is about 2 inches thick. While an uncured laminate obviously will not be that thick, the heat of the curing reaction should not be ignored. For example, in bonding interior components to the hull of our boat, *Sea Sparrow*, I would put unused resin from each batch into a waste container as soon as gelation started. On one occasion, I created a dangerous situation by unthinkingly pouring a small amount of waste acetone into the same container. The acetone very quickly began boiling from the heat given off by even that small accumulation of resin curing in that container. Even left by itself, waste resin can be a hazard; the heat given off as it cures can be enough to start the waste resin burning.

Gel Coats

Gel coat has two principal functions: One is cosmetic—to provide a smooth, colored surface; the other is more utilitarian—to resist migration of water into the laminate. To satisfy the cosmetic function, only premium-grade resins are normally used for gel coat. Special effort is made, for example, to keep the resin color free so that less pigment is needed to obtain the desired finished color. To satisfy the utilitarian function, gel coat resins generally are formulated to be more water resistant than laminating resins.

The importance of gel coat water resistance cannot be overstated. Perhaps the one shortcoming of fiber glass boat construction that continues to plague both the industry and boat owners alike is the problem of gel coat blistering below the waterline (see Chapter 10). These blisters appear to be directly related to the migration of water through the gel coat. To enhance water resistance, industry opinion is that gel coat resins used for boat construction should be made using isophthalic acid. By some estimates, the use of isophthalic acid adds about 10 percent to the builder's gel coat cost, but the downstream savings in terms of the increased resistance to surface blistering is considered well worth that added cost. Some gel coat manufacturers also use neopentyl glycol (NPG) in the alcohol component of the resin to get even better water resistance as well as increased toughness and resistance to weathering. The use of the NPG also increases the gel coat resin costs; NPG is 10 to 15 percent more expensive than the propylene glycol it replaces. Usually these gel coat resins are specifically promoted as "isophthalic NPG gel coat resins."

Most often, of course, we think of gel coat only on the outside of a boat. However, gel coat should be applied also to the inside of the hull laminate, at least in the bilges after all frames, stringers, and structural bulkheads have been installed, but before the cabin or cockpit soles are put down. One purpose of the gel coat in the bilge is the same as the gel coat on the hull's outer surface, to protect from migration of water into the laminate; another, however, is to make it easier to keep the bilges clean by providing a smooth surface less likely to trap grime and so forth.

Laminating Resins

The key functions of laminating resins are structural. Whereas the gel coat layer should be only about 20 to 22 mils thick, the laminate structure—including the fiber reinforcement—may range up to 2 inches or more in thickness, depending upon the size of the boat and the specific part of the hull being considered.

Laminating resins are formulated to soak into the reinforcing fabrics, encapsulate the individual fibers, and form a tough plastic matrix; however, the resin must also perform other functions. For example, it must adhere strongly to the gel coat and provide a strong chemical and mechanical bond between successive layers of the laminate so that the entire structure forms a single, unified structure. It must be sufficiently resilient that it will not fail from the inevitable flexing the structure will experience in use. And it should be formulated for easy use—often by relatively unskilled labor—under a wide variety of working conditions.

Although resin producers market a large number of "different" formulations to accomplish all of these objectives, three basic varieties of polyester laminating resins are most common: those made with orthophthalic acid, those with isophthalic acid, and those made using a chemical called DCPD, an abbreviation for the longer chemical name, dicyclopentadiene. Of course, any individual resin may also be a blend of these various ingredients.

Orthophthalic laminating resins are the commonly used general-purpose laminating resins. They are, in the words of resin experts, good general-purpose resins for the marine industry.

Isophthalic laminating resins offer increased water and chemical resistance; they also are somewhat tougher resins. Use of isophthalic laminating resins, however, adds about 10 percent to the builder's resin costs and there is question whether the small increase in performance justifies the added cost. As a result, few builders use isophthalic laminating resins.

It should also be noted that the major producer of isophthalic acid in the United States has conducted tests that it says demonstrate that using both an isophthalic gel coat and an isophthalic laminating resin can prevent gel coat blistering. Some resin manufacturers and boat builders question the validity of those tests because of the conditions under which they are conducted. In an effort to accelerate the blistering process (speed up the aging process), test panels are exposed to water at 149°F, almost twice the water temperature boats will normally encounter, even in tropical waters.

DCPD is a relatively new wrinkle in resin technology that has given rise to so-called "low-profile laminating resins." These resins are new enough that experts do not really know at this writing exactly what kind of polymer is formed by these resins.

Although DCPD is not an acid, it can be used to replace or dilute the "saturated" acid component of the resin. Because DCPD is very reactive, these resins reach a complete cure more quickly, offering two advantages: Their use speeds up the laminating process and the faster cure helps reduce "pattern show-through," a problem in which the weave of the reinforcing fabric shows through the gel coat, compromising the aesthetic quality of the hull. These resins also shrink very little compared to standard general-purpose laminating resins—possibly a mixed blessing. While the low shrinkage is thought to help prevent pattern show-through, it also may make it more difficult to remove hulls from the molds. The usual 7 to 8 percent shrinkage of the orthophthalic and isophthalic laminating resins contributes to the ease of removal from the mold. Use of DCPD also may involve other compromise as well: DCPD resins tend to be more brittle and they do not wet out (saturate) reinforcing fabrics as easily as many general-purpose resins. In addition, there are reports of laminates made using DCPD resins not adhering well to the gel coat, possibly because the outer layers of the laminate were not adequately wet out as the hull was laid up.

Epoxy Resins

From a performance viewpoint, epoxy resins are generally superior to polyesters: They are stronger, tougher, have superior chemical resistance initially, and adhere to almost anything. In use, the superior adhesive properties of epoxy resins sometimes offers an advantage when applying reinforcing materials to vertical or overhead surfaces. But epoxy resins also have certain disadvantages: They are at least twice as expensive as polyester resins and may be three to four times as expensive when the cost of the curing agent is included. They are also more difficult to use, no small consideration in an industry in which laying up a hull is often an entry-level job for unskilled labor.

Unlike the example of polyester resins in which all of the resin's ingredients are packaged together from the outset, epoxies consist of two parts that are kept separated until use. One part consists of a goop containing short-chain polymers that will form the backbone of the cured resin. The second part contains a curing agent that reacts chemically to form the cross-links which tie the polymer chains into a hard, tough plastic matrix. The curing process for an epoxy resin is inherently a slower reaction than that for polyester resins. The cure provides a gradual increase in the viscosity (thickness or stiffness) of the resin, with less heat given off. Usually, the curing agent represents between 10 and 40 percent of the final chemical structure of the resin.

Because of the cost of epoxy resins and the large amount of resin used in fiber glass construction (about two-thirds of the weight of a typical solid fiber glass hull is resin), few fiber-reinforced boats are built using an epoxy for the laminating resin. However, epoxy resins are sometimes used to lay up smaller high-stress components of a boat. They are usually the resins of choice today for boats using cold-molded wood construction (see Chapter 5), and they are sometimes used to bond components to the fiber glass hull because of their superior adhesive characteristics (Table 1).

Vinylester Resins

Although few boats have been built using vinylester resins, the increased use of exotic reinforcing materials and the continual quest for lighter, stronger hulls for racing enthusiasts suggest that we may see more of these resins used in boat construction in the future.

The vinylester resins were developed for use in chemical plants where corrosion resistance is important. They are a cross between epoxies and polyesters. An oversimplified, but essentially correct, description is that they are made from an epoxy resin backbone but use styrene to form the cross-links that tie the polymer chains together. This "marriage" of technology has resulted in a resin that shows the ease of handling characteristic of polyester resins and some of the improved performance characteristic of the epoxies at a cost much closer to polyesters than epoxies.

For example, the cure is initiated by using MEK peroxide and is characterized by the same gelation process found in the polyesters. At the same time, like epoxies, the vinylester resins provide better adhesion and show better "elongation" proper-

Table 1   Characteristics of Major Resin Types

Polyester	*Epoxy*	*Vinylester*
Uses initiator to begin cure; initiator does not become part of cured resin matrix	Requires catalyst for cure; catalyst becomes part of cured resin matrix	Falls between epoxy and polyester; uses initiator to begin cure; initiator does not become part of cured resin matrix
Changes from liquid to gel suddenly after 10 to 20 minutes	Slow cure with gradual thickening from liquid to solid	Changes from liquid to gel suddenly after 10 to 20 minutes
Cures to tough, strong FRP laminate after several days	Cures to tougher, stronger FRP laminate than polyester, but at two to four times the cost	Cures to tougher, less brittle FRP laminate than polyester resins, but less tough than epoxy; about one and a half times the cost of polyester resins
Relatively easy to use	More difficult to use than polyester	Similar to polyester in use difficulty

ties (i.e., they will stretch more in use) than polyesters. Typical elongation (stretch) of a vinylester resin is from 4 to 5 percent. Isophthalic polyester resins show elongation of about 2 percent. Elongation of orthophthalic polyester resins is from 1.5 to 2 percent. This means vinylester resins are tougher and less brittle than polyester resins. It also means they will withstand greater strain before failure, a combination of properties that makes them particularly suitable for use with reinforcing fabrics made of new high-strength fibers. With all of these advantages, one can reasonably ask why vinylesters are not used more widely. One reason is quite simple: They have not yet been widely "discovered" by the boating industry. Another reason is equally fundamental: cost. Although vinylester resins are significantly less expensive than epoxies, they still cost about twice as much as the best polyester laminating resins.

REINFORCING MATERIALS

In 1962 and again in 1971, Owens Corning obtained sample sections from the hull of one of the original 40-foot fiber glass patrol boats built for the U.S. Coast Guard in 1952. These samples were used to evaluate the performance of the hull laminates. For all practical purposes, the boat was in continual Coast Guard service from commissioning in 1952 until it was retired in 1971. There was no evidence of deterioration in the fiber glass hull in the 10 years between the time the boat was constructed and the first sample was taken in 1962. Moreover, tests demonstrated that there was no deterioration in physical properties of the fiber glass hull in the 10 years between 1962 and 1971. However, comparison of the physical properties of the hull samples with typical laminates made using conventional 1970s materials provided a dramatic demonstration of the improvements in fiber glass technology that took place between 1952 and 1971. The more modern laminates provided from two to four times better performance in tests of strength and stiffness.

One key to the improved performance of laminates, of course, has been the progress made with resins. However, improvements in reinforcing materials have also been of major importance: for example, introduction of a wider variety of conventional fiber glass reinforcing fabrics and development of fabric treatments that enhance both penetration of resins into the fabric and the bond between the resin and the fiber surface. In addition, development of new fiber materials for use in reinforcing fabrics is now leading to still further increases in the performance of fiber-reinforced plastics in the marine industry.

Conventional Fiber Glass Materials

In the early 1950s, builders had little choice in fiber glass reinforcing fabrics. They came in only two forms: a smooth fiber glass cloth and a feltlike fabric known as chopped strand mat. Today the variety of fiber glass materials seems to grow almost yearly as individual builders work with suppliers to develop reinforcement materials designed specifically to handle the structural requirements of their boats. Moreover, two types of glass fibers are available: One, called *E-glass,* is used in 99 percent of marine products made of fiber glass; the other, known as *S-glass,* was developed for the aerospace industry and will be described later in this chapter.

The following are conventional fiber glass reinforcing materials in use by the marine industry as of this writing.

Chopped strand mat is a loose feltlike material most often used in one of two weights, ¾ of an ounce per square foot or, more commonly, 1.5 ounces per square foot (Photo 2). Chopped strand mat is made by laying down a thin layer of glass fibers about 2 inches long, treating them with a chemical binder, and then pressing the "raw" mat between rollers. Because of the inherent difficulty in controlling product consistency in this production process, the weight of mat fabrics may vary from the standard (for example, 1.5 ounces per square foot) by as much as 20 percent in either direction.

Chopped strand mat is usually used for the first layer behind the gel coat and between layers of coarser woven fabric to provide a better bonding surface between laminates and to build laminate thickness. It is sometimes also used to bond components to the hull. Because the fibers lie in all directions, lay-ups made using only chopped strand mat tend to show uniform stiffness and strength in all directions. However, such laminates have relatively low flexural and impact strength because the laminate contains only short fibers. In addition, laminates made using only chopped strand mat have a comparatively low percentage of glass content—usually in the range of 25 to 30 percent fiber glass—because an excess of resin is needed to wet the mat thoroughly. This factor also is related to the comparatively lower strength of laminates made using only chopped strand mat. It should be noted that up to a level of about 55 percent, the higher glass content means a stronger laminate. Above 55 percent fiber glass content, laminates tend to be resin starved and the laminate performance is reduced.

2. Chopped strand mat. (Photo courtesy of Owens Corning Fiberglas)

Roving is essentially a heavy yarn bearing a resemblance to baling twine, but made of continuous glass fibers (Photo 3). Roving is packaged on large spools and is the least expensive form of fiber glass reinforcement. It is used in three principal ways: (1) It is run through a "chopper gun" (see below) for a semiautomated lay-up process called "chop," (2) lengths of roving are used to fill in crevices or to provide extra reinforcement in one direction at specific high-stress areas, and (3) continuous strands of roving are used to make heavy woven and nonwoven reinforcing fabrics.

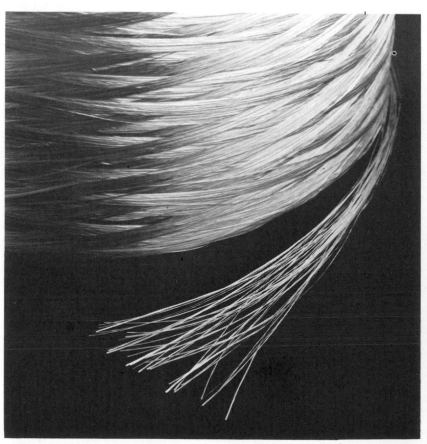

3. Roving for use in a chopper gun. (Photo courtesy of Owens Corning Fiberglas)

Chop is a technique for applying chopped strand (roving) reinforcement by spraying the chopped fibers and resin simultaneously onto a mold. In some respects, the "chopper gun" resembles a paint spray nozzle in which the resin and catalyst are fed by hose from large tanks and mixed as the spraying takes place. A dye, usually in the catalyst, helps the applicator see where the resin is being sprayed. Attached to the "gun" are devices that feed from one to four strands of roving into a cutting mechanism that "chops" the roving into short lengths. As they are chopped, the cut fibers are blown into the resin spray and onto the laminate surface. Applying chopped fibers in this manner saves builders money in materials and time over hand lay-up of a mat layer. The evenness and quality of chopper gun laminates is heavily dependent upon the skill of the chopper gun operator, as is, for example, the quality of a spray paint job. A competent chopper gun operator obtains an evenness of distribution of the chopped roving that is within the ±20 percent range accepted for production of mat fabrics. A competent operator also obtains glass-to-resin ratios in the same 25 to 30 percent range expected for laminates of chopped or continuous strand mat, but usually at the lower end of that range.

Woven roving is a coarsely woven fabric in which strands of roving are at right angles to each other (Photo 4). Generally, about 55 percent of the glass fibers run in one direction and 45 percent in the other. This means that the greatest strength of the woven roving lies along the axis with the heaviest fiber content. The lowest strength lies at an angle of 45 degrees to the fiber strands (i.e., diagonally to the weave).

Woven roving was introduced in the early 1960s to replace the lighter weight fiber glass cloths used up to that time. Today woven roving used in conjunction with chop or mat is the principal reinforcement fabric used in construction of fiber glass boats longer than 20 feet. Its coarse weave, however, means it cannot be used next to gel coat without the woven pattern showing through. In addition, the coarse weave generally makes it desirable to use a layer of mat or chop between layers of woven roving to help ensure a good bond between layers, because the mat layer will conform readily to the hills and valleys of the surface of the woven fabrics. Laminates of 100 percent woven roving will have a relatively high glass content—usually in the range of 40 to 55 percent. A typical boat laminate of alternating layers of 1.5-ounce mat and 24-ounce woven roving usually will have a glass content between 30 and 40 percent, though it may be as much as 45 percent in a well-done lay-up. Use of a ¾-ounce mat usually will result in a higher glass content in the finished laminate.

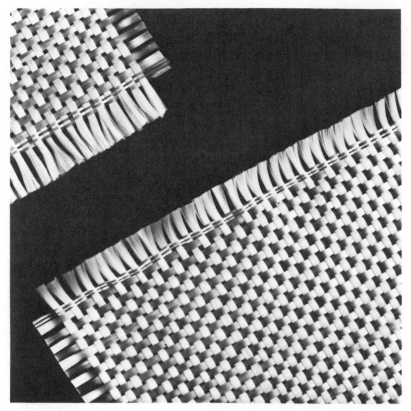

4. Woven roving. (Photo courtesy of Owens Corning Fiberglas)

The most commonly used woven roving weighs 24 ounces per square yard. Other weights of woven roving—typically 40 or 18 ounces per square yard—also are available. The 40-ounce fabric is generally used for very large boats and for building up strength and thickness with fewer laminations in smaller boats, for example, in reinforcing the keel area of a sailboat. The 18-ounce fabric tends to be used in thinner laminates, often with ¾-ounce mat between the woven layers.

Some builders are turning to 18-ounce woven roving in place of 24-ounce fabric, because it is easier to work with. One builder, for example, says his tests show that the heavier fabric does not get fully wet out during the laminating process in his plant. As a result, the laminate is starved for resin and does not achieve its full strength potential. By using an 18-ounce fabric, he says, the same amount of resin gives better saturation of the reinforcement. The result is a lighter laminate that, according to his tests, have physical performance properties equal to the test results obtained on laminates being produced in his shop using 24-ounce woven roving.

It should be noted that 24-ounce woven roving properly wet out normally will provide significantly greater reinforcement on a layer-for-layer basis than 18-ounce fabric, simply because there is a third more fiber in the reinforcing fabric. The lighter weight of the 18-ounce woven roving, however, can be compensated for by adding one or more layers of fabric to the lay-up schedule. In this case, some builders believe the ease of wetting out the lighter fabric and the opportunity to use ¾-ounce mat between the woven layers enable them to produce a stronger laminate.

Boat cloth is a relatively lightweight smoothly woven cloth of fiber glass. In the early years of fiber glass boat construction, boat cloth and mat were the only fiber glass reinforcing materials available. However, the light weight of the fabric required a large number of layers to build up thickness. The relatively high percentage of mat in such laminates contributed to a comparatively low glass content. Test panels from one of the 40-foot patrol boats built for the Coast Guard in 1952, for example, showed a 24 percent glass content, less than would usually be obtained with a 100 percent mat construction today. In the early 1970s, some builders still used fiber glass cloth as the final layer in the lay-up to provide a "finished" appearance. Today, however, comparatively little boat cloth is used in the boating industry—mostly for interior moldings requiring a smooth surface finish, light weight, and a higher strength-to-weight ratio than is attainable using mat alone. Examples include shower stalls and fuel and water tanks.

Fabmat or Bi-Ply are two trademarks for combination fabrics consisting of a layer of woven roving chemically bonded to a layer of mat (Photo 5). Such materials are more expensive than equivalent quantities of mat and woven roving purchased separately. In addition, the combination materials are harder to use—particularly for beginners—because it is more difficult to work the resin completely through the thick fabric. However, use of combination fabrics can save lay-up time, particularly when pieces must be cut and fit—for example, as in bonding bulkheads to the hull—because they allow application of two layers at a time.

5. Bi-Ply fabric combines chopped strand mat with woven roving so that both layers of the laminate can be applied in one operation. (Photo courtesy of Owens Corning Fiberglas)

Unidirectional roving is a fabric in which 90 percent or more of the fibers run in the same direction. Essentially, unidirectional roving consists of a series of strands of roving laid out next to each other and held together in a fabric by a fiber glass or polyester yarn knit or stitched at right angles to the rovings at intervals of a few inches. Some unidirectional rovings are made to so-called "aircraft specifications." These have virtually all of the reinforcing fibers running in the same direction. These fabrics are held together by narrow bands of fiber running across the fabric at intervals of about an inch and a half and glued in place with an adhesive binder.

The rationale behind the use of unidirectional roving is

straightforward. Laminates made using unidirectional roving tend to provide at least equal strength but weigh less than comparable laminates made using typical woven roving lay-ups. Three key factors are involved: (1) Because most of the fibers in unidirectional roving lie right next to each other and run in the same direction, it is possible to obtain a higher density and more uniform distribution of fibers in the fabric; (2) the fibers in woven fabrics tend to break each other because of the over/under configuration; and (3) because most of the fibers run in a single direction, the boat designer can use his reinforcement materials more efficiently by orienting the unidirectional roving along the lines of stress. For example, a given high-stress area that could be adequately served by two layers of unidirectional roving may require three or four laminates of woven roving (which has only about 55 percent of its fibers running in one direction) to provide needed reinforcement.

It is also usually possible to save weight when using unidirectional roving: Fewer laminates are required to provide the needed strength and, a lighter weight mat can be used between layers of unidirectional roving than is needed between layers of woven roving. (In a custom yard, where close control over laminating practice is possible, use of mat between layers of unidirectional roving can be eliminated entirely, with still more weight savings.) However, unidirectional fabrics may be difficult to lay up. The density of the glass fibers in the fabric and the fact that nearly all of the fibers run in a single direction make unidirectional roving somewhat stiffer than a woven fabric. As a result, it may not conform as easily to the contours of the structure. Wetting out the fabric, on the other hand, is not usually a problem, despite the increased density of the fibers; in fact, the increased fiber density tends to improve the wicking action of the fabric, assisting resin penetration throughout.

Bidirectional and triaxial rovings are fabrics in which two or three layers of unidirectional roving have been placed one on top of the other so that the fibers in each layer run in a different direction than fibers in the other layers. The multiple layers are stitched together using a special knitting machine to form a single fabric. These materials are said to provide opportunity for boat designers to engineer the properties of the reinforcing material more closely than is otherwise possible, because the layers of reinforcement are oriented to each other in production of the fabric rather than in the less controlled environment of the lay-up process.

Technically, woven roving is "bidirectional," that is, the fibers in the fabric run in two directions. In practice, however, the term *bidirectional roving* usually refers to a non-woven fabric made up of layers of unidirectional roving. Triaxial roving refers to a nonwoven fabric in which the layers are oriented in three different directions. Such materials are new and are used by few production boat builders. Like the unidirectional rovings from which they are constructed, such fabrics offer builders opportunity to construct lighter, stronger hulls and decks. Builders may find them more difficult to use, because these fabrics tend to be stiffer than woven roving, but use of different stitching techniques and, possibly, stitching with a stretch yarn is expected to make these fabrics less stiff. As is the case with unidirectional roving, the increased density of the fibers increases the wicking action of these fabrics, with the result that Proform, Inc., one manufacturer, claims it is easier to wet out a 34-ounce triaxial fabric than it is to wet out a conventional 24-ounce woven roving. The experience of some builders runs counter to that claim, however.

"Exotic" Reinforcing Materials

While well over 95 percent of the fiber-reinforced boats built today are made using conventional fiber glass reinforcing materials, there is a small, growing use of so-called "exotic" materials—"exotic" because they are expensive; because they have been used pr   ipally in highly specialized aerospace applications; becaus   e fabrics are specially crafted for high-strength, lightweight ap plicat ons; and because most of us simply do not know much about them.

These materials have most often been used by the marine industry for construction of custom racing boats—power and sail—because they offer the same strength as conventional materials for less weight. When pounds can be translated into added miles per hour or seconds faster along a course line, the savings can be important.

More recently, however, these materials have started finding their way into production boats. Some builders have begun offering the use of exotic reinforcing materials as an option, thereby letting customers purchase higher performance without the expense of a custom boat. Others are looking at these materials to help save weight, giving their boats just enough of a boost in performance to provide a marketing edge over their competition. And some too have discovered the marketing power of exotic fibers. These builders are using one or more exotic materials at various places in their boats at least in part to capitalize on the appeal that mere use of these reinforcements has for the buying public.

S-Glass is a special glass formulation developed by Owens Corning specifically for the aerospace industry to provide high-performance glass fiber reinforcement for FRP composites. S-Glass provides 30 to 40 percent higher tensile strength, impact strength, and flexural strength on an equal weight basis than conventional E-glass fibers. The cost of that improved performance, however, is high. There are two grades of S-glass: S-1 is produced to very stringent specifications for aerospace use and is said to be "very expensive"; S-2, which is the grade used in the marine industry, meets less stringent specifications but provides the same high level of performance as its sister grade. The cost of the S-2 grade of S-glass is three to four times the cost of conventional E-glass materials.

Kevlar 49 is an organic fiber widely used in the aerospace industry but gradually finding increased use in boat construction. Chemically, Kevlar is similar to nylon. Its physical properties, however, are sufficiently different from those of nylon that a new generic classification, aramid, was adopted for these fibers.

Kevlar has a characteristic golden color; some wags have noted it also has a golden price. However, pound for pound, Kevlar is the strongest reinforcing fiber available. It weighs little more than half as much as conventional fiber glass, yet fibers of Kevlar are 50 percent stronger and 80 percent stiffer than glass fibers of the same size. In addition, Kevlar shows less stretch than fiber glass. From a practical viewpoint, the strength, stiff-ness, and light weight of Kevlar enable a builder to lay up either a stronger hull or one of strength similar to a comparable fiber glass hull, but with significant weight savings, by direct substi-tution of woven roving or unidirectional roving of Kevlar for comparable fiber glass materials. It should be noted, however, that even when Kevlar is used, a significant portion of the lam-inate consists of fiber glass chopped strand mat.

In practice, Kevlar generally is used to save weight. For example, a 34-foot commercial fishing boat in which woven roving of Kevlar was substituted for fiber glass woven roving weighed in about 2,450 pounds lighter (12 percent) than a sis-ter ship made using all fiber glass materials. It should be noted, however, that the potential weight savings from use of Kevlar varies with boat size. In smaller boats, the savings is limited to the difference in weight between the Kevlar and fiber glass woven rovings plus, possibly, the opportunity to use ¾-ounce mat with the woven Kevlar fabric in place of the 1.5-ounce mat required with the heavier fiber glass roving. On larger boats, which may have several layers of woven roving in their hulls, the greater stiffness and strength of the Kevlar reinforcement may make it possible to eliminate one or more laminations as well as to use lighter weight mat layers, increasing potential weight savings by reducing both the glass and resin content of the hull. Boats under 30 to 35 feet, however, usually do not have enough layers of woven roving to make it possible to reduce the number of laminations. In any case, except where the num-ber of laminations is being reduced, the Kevlar fabrics should be substituted for all layers of the fiber glass woven roving. Merely replacing only one of two or three layers of fiber glass woven roving with Kevlar fabric only adds cost; it will benefit the boat little.

Kevlar is not without its disadvantages, of course, or it would be in much wider use. One disadvantage designers must take into consideration, particularly in sailboat design, is the relatively low compressive strength of Kevlar—lower than that of conventional fiber glass as well as of other "exotic" materials. A second disadvantage stems from the stiffness of Kevlar, which makes it more difficult to bend these fabrics around sharp angles; the fabric wants to straighten out. A third disadvantage for its use in production line boat building is the increased attention to detail required for laying up Kevlar reinforcing fabrics. The difficulty occurs because of the fiber's solid gold color. When fiber glass materials are fully saturated with resin, they become transparent and the workers know the fabric is fully saturated. Although the color of Kevlar changes to a deeper gold as it is wet out, the fabric remains opaque, making it more difficult for workers to determine whether it has been fully saturated with resin during the lay-up process. The best way to avoid this problem is to wet out the fabric from the bottom so that any dry spots will occur on the upper surface, where they would be readily visible. This is done by following the standard good laminating procedure of applying resin to the laminate, laying the Kevlar fabric onto the resin, and then rolling it out, working the resin up through the fabric.

Still another disadvantage Kevlar carries is that of cost. One builder of powerboats in the 25-foot range says he offers an option of using Kevlar in the hull for an additional cost of about $100 per foot of hull length. A more general rule of thumb is that use of Kevlar in the hull of a standard 30- to 35-foot boat adds about 15 percent to the boat's total cost. In the example of the 34-foot commercial fishing boat mentioned earlier, the added cost was about $6,500. In the case of that particular boat, tests have shown that the increased cost from the use of Kevlar can be recouped in about two years (about 3,000 hours of operation) from fuel savings due to the boat's lower weight. For pleasure boat use, where 3,000 hours is likely to represent more nearly 10 years of use, that added cost is more difficult to justify in terms of fuel savings at present fuel costs. As a result, the use of Kevlar generally has to be justified in terms of performance—whether the boat will go faster. Moreover, there also are specialized applications for Kevlar in which the incremental cost is small but savings in weight or increased safety make that cost worthwhile. Most such applications involve use of a core material and will be discussed in subsequent chapters.

Carbon (graphite) fibers are lightweight organic fibers that find specialized application because of their exceptional stiffness, or resistance to bending, and their high compressive strength

(Photo 6). The modulus (stiffness) of "high-strength" carbon fibers is about 80 percent greater than that of Kevlar 49 and about three times that of conventional fiber glass materials for fibers of equal size. Moreover, carbon fibers have a strength rating equal to that of S-glass and about 85 percent that of Kevlar, again for fibers of equal size. Although carbon fibers are

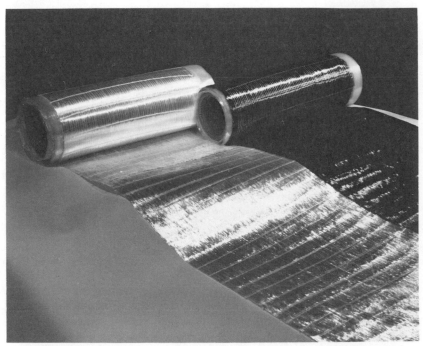

6. Unidirectional fabrics of fiber glass and of carbon (graphite) fiber demonstrate the lengthwise orientation of the reinforcing fibers. The transverse stitching serves only to hold the fabric together. (Photo courtesy of Orcon, Inc.)

about 20 percent heavier than Kevlar, they are only about two-thirds the weight of fiber glass. Importantly, however, carbon fibers are relatively brittle. As a result, composites using carbon fiber reinforcement have relatively low impact resistance.

Because of this mix of properties, the use of carbon fiber reinforcement is usually highly specialized. In the marine industry, carbon fibers generally have been used where light

weight and stiffness are of primary importance. On some racing sailboats, carbon fiber reinforced tubes have been used for
rudder shafts to save weight aft, though with some notable failures because the tubes apparently were not engineered adequately for the forces encountered. On some boats, a layer of
undirectional roving of carbon fiber is used to help stiffen longitudinal reinforcing stringers in the hull. On sailboats using
unstayed masts, the masts may be made of fiber-reinforced
plastic using carbon fiber reinforcement, again because of its
light weight and exceptional resistance to bending, or stiffness
(Table 2). This application is described in some detail in Chapter 12.

Hybrid reinforcing materials are fabrics made using two or more
different reinforcing fibers. Examples include unidirectional
roving consisting of both Kevlar and S-glass, or of Kevlar and
carbon, in the same fabric. Such hybrids are fabricated to combine the advantages of each fiber into a single reinforcing fabric. For example, Orcon Corporation produces a hybrid
unidirectional roving of Kevlar and carbon fiber designed to
combine the high compressive strength and stiffness of carbon

Table 2   Reinforcing Fibers Used in Boat Construction

E-Glass	Conventional fiber glass material; used in about 99 percent of all *fiber glass* boat construction
S-Glass	Special glass formula developed for the aerospace indus-try; provides from 30 to 40 percent higher tensile strength, impact strength, and flexural strength then E-glass on an equal weight basis
Kevlar	A man-made organic fiber, pound for pound the strongest of all reinforcing fibers available; about 50 percent stronger than conventional glass fibers at one-half the weight
Carbon	Organic man-made fiber with exceptional resistance to bending; stiffness is up to 80 percent greater than Kevlar and five times that of conventional glass fiber
Hybrids	Usually blends of Kevlar and S-glass or of Kevlar and car-bon fiber to obtain best characteristics of both fibers

fibers with the high tensile strength and impact resistance of Kevlar. Another such hybrid is a unidirectional roving of 80 percent (by volume) Kevlar and 20 percent S-glass. This fabric is said to have exceptionally high impact strength—more than one would expect from the performance of each fiber type alone—because of an apparent synergistic effect from use of that small percentage of S-glass with Kevlar. Ironically, the S-glass apparently was blended with the Kevlar initially to help workers using the material know when the Kevlar fabric was saturated with resin, because, as noted earlier, the glass fibers become transparent when saturated. The improved performance of the hybrid was an unexpected bonus.

Preimpregnated Reinforcing Materials

The need in the aerospace industry to engineer fiber-reinforced plastic materials to specific high-performance standards has spawned the development of fabrics called "prepregs." Essentially, these are fabrics of fiber glass or other reinforcing materials that have been saturated with resin at the factory, the cure started, and the cure then stopped—usually by refrigeration—before the prepreg has been shipped to the boat or aircraft builder. Although most prepreg materials are made of woven or unidirectional fabrics, some prepreg mat is also available. The cost of prepregs is about double the cost of materials for a comparable wet lay-up. When using woven roving prepregs, laminates of between 50 and 55 percent fiber glass content are attainable consistently. A glass content much above 55 percent results in a porosity problem because the system is resin starved.

Prepreg materials resemble a waxed fabric in appearance and feel. The fabric is usually kept under refrigeration until being placed in the mold. When the lay-up is completed, the mold and the entire laminate are placed in an oven and heated to about 250°F for several hours to bring about the cure. Prepregs are used in conjunction with vacuum bag molding techniques. The vacuum bag system is needed to compact the lay-up and assist the resin flow. Vacuum bagging will be discussed in Chapter 3.

Few production boat builders use prepregs at this writing, but some are looking into the possibility. One builder who does use prepregs is Force Engineering in Sarasota, Florida. Force uses fiber glass prepregs for construction of its Stiletto catamaran, and prepregs of either fiber glass or Kevlar to fabricate parts or even complete hulls and decks for other boat builders.

Prepregs offer three principal advantages: They are a pre-testable system, glass-to-resin ratios can be guaranteed, and builders have much better control over the characteristics of the resin system. All three advantages exist because prepregs are produced in a factory under closely controlled conditions, a distinct contrast to the more common marriage of resin and fiber, which takes place in the open lay-up shop of the boat builder. There are also two secondary advantages to the use of prepregs: They eliminate the mess involved in conventional laminating procedures and they do away with possible problems involving styrene vapors. Along with these advantages, however, prepregs carry one principal disadvantage: They have a limited shelf life. At room temperature, the shelf life is only 1 or 2 weeks; at 40°F, shelf life is about 3 months; at 0°F, shelf life is 6 months. There is, of course, a straightforward means of accommodating the shelf-life limitations of prepregs: keeping the prepreg materials in a cold storage room and maintaining close control of inventory so that they are used on a first-in, first-out basis.

3

The Basic FRP Hull
Solid Laminates in
a Female Mold

Traditionally, boat hulls have been built from the inside out. In conventional wood hull construction, for example, timbers are laid to form the keel and stem. Ribs are cut or bent to shape, set in place, and then tied together by a series of "stringers" running fore and aft along the inside of the structure. Finally, the hull is planked—a process that not only requires cutting, bending, and fitting individual planks over the ribs, but which also means fastening the planks with screws (or nails) and then putting wood plugs over each countersunk screwhead. In a carvel-built hull, the seams between the planks must be caulked using a loose cotton rope and seam compound. Regardless, the entire hull has to be sanded and painted before it is said to be finished. In the case of a 35-foot boat, this entire process generally takes weeks just to complete the wood hull, and longer in a small yard with few employees.

Today the time required to build a hull to the same design in fiber glass using a female mold is more likely to be measured in days, particularly in one of the larger boat plants working on two or three shifts. By the time the first wood hull has been built, several identical fiber glass hulls will be out of the mold and the first one may be approaching the end of the production line.

The steps in molding a fiber glass hull are strikingly few and they progress from the outside in: The builder sprays the gel coat resin over the mold; after letting the gel coat cure, he begins laying up the reinforcing materials and plastic laminating resin. Some structural framework may be added later, but often the normal complement of interior bulkheads, floor members, cabin sole, and furnishings can serve as structural framework if the various components are bonded securely to the hull. Moreover, little finishing work is usually needed on the outer surface of the hull; it comes out of the mold almost ready for the show-room floor (Photo 7).

The actual process of building a production fiber glass hull, of course, is more complex than described. The mold itself must be constructed and, depending upon the boat design, one of several different mold configurations may be required. In building the hull itself, there are different methods for apply-

7. As a newly laminated FRP hull is removed from its female mold, the surface finish can be almost boat-show perfect, a stark contrast to custom or wood boat construction, where many hours of careful hand fairing are needed to provide a finished appearance. (Photo by Susan Roberts)

ing the reinforcing materials and even the choice of laminating resins may influence actual lay-up procedures.

MOLDS

Virtually all fiber glass production boats are made using a female mold. We have all made such molds at one time or another: a hand print in fresh concrete, a footprint in wet sand at the beach, a tire track in soft ground or fresh snow. Each of these was a female mold, or could have been. We could have used the imprinted images to cast an identical likeness of the palm of our hand, the bottom of our foot, or even the tread from our car's tire. It is a technique crime investigators since Sherlock Holmes have used to good advantage many times.

The hand print, footprint, or tire tread mold we have made so casually was created by pressing our hand, foot, or tire into a soft medium. Although at some large plants, hull molds are recessed into the factory floor and look, for all intents and purposes, as if a boat hull had been pressed into the floor, that is not how boat molds are produced.

Most boat molds are made using conventional fiber glass materials. The mold begins with something called a "plug." In the case of the footprint in the sand, the plug was someone's foot; in the case of a boat mold, the plug often is a custom-made boat hull (to be discussed in Chapter 4). It may also be a facsimile of a boat hull. In either case, construction of the plug is critical. Any flaws in the plug will be transferred to the mold and, in turn, to every boat made from that mold. As a result, great care is taken to obtain the best possible finish on the plug, with free use of fillers to make the surface as fair as men's skills can make it. If the plug is a facsimile to be discarded after the mold is completed, this use of fillers causes no hardship. If an actual boat hull is used for the plug, however, excessive use of fillers to fair out the hull may become a problem to the person who purchases the boat made from that hull. After a few years, the fillers may begin to come off the hull, requiring a costly face-lift.

Once the plug has been completed, it becomes a master copy

with which to make the fiber glass female mold. Its surface is waxed carefully so that the plug can be removed easily from the completed mold without damaging the surface finish. Top-quality gel coat resin—called "tool-quality" gel coat in the trade—is sprayed over the plug, usually at twice the thickness used for a boat hull. A series of laminates is then applied over the gel coat. Some builders use the more expensive, but somewhat tougher, isophthalic tool-quality laminating resins for constructing molds. In all cases before the plug is removed, a framework of steel and/or wood is constructed around the mold—becoming a part of the mold itself—to ensure that the mold cannot change shape (Photo 8). Once the plug has been pulled, the mold surface is checked carefully for blemishes, all of which must be repaired before the mold is put into service

8. A tubular steel framework is commonly constructed around the exterior of an FRP boat mold to help ensure that the mold retains its proper shape. (Photo by Susan Roberts)

or they will be passed along to every hull pulled from the mold. Builders who expect to construct a large number (hundreds) of boats from the same design often make a new plug called a "glass master" from the mold before putting it into the production line. The glass master is used later to make additional molds of that hull design.

The cost in 1982 of producing a single mold for an 18- to 30-foot hull, including the cost of producing the plug and a glass master, ran from $50,000 to $100,000, according to one large builder of powerboats. Molds for larger boats may run several times that amount. The cost of molds, of course, must be amortized over the production run for that hull design. A builder normally can expect to produce several dozen to several hundred hulls from a single mold, depending upon factors ranging from the quality of gel coat used to make the mold to shop conditions when the mold was made to the care it receives after being put into service. Often high-volume builders maximize production runs from hull molds by designing different deck and interior arrangements around existing hulls, by changing a sailboat's rig or a motorboat's power option from inboard to inboard / outboard, or by simply changing hull and deck color schemes and trim. Sometimes, too, molds are sold to another builder, who then develops his own variant of the same boat.

One-Piece and Multipiece Molds

Most boat hulls are produced in one-piece molds. The hull's lines have been designed so that the completed hull can be lifted out of the mold with little difficulty. This is the least costly and easiest system to use. Sometimes, however, space limitations may dictate using a two-piece mold, particularly on very large molds. For example, if there is not enough overhead clearance to lift a hull from the mold, the builder may choose a system that enables him to move the two halves of the mold away from the sides of the finished hull.

The use of a two-piece mold may also be dictated by boat design. For example, reverse transoms and tumblehome require two-piece molds; otherwise, the builder could not get the boat out of the mold. In the case of a reverse transom, usually only the transom section of the mold would be removable. If the sides of the hull turn back in toward the center of the boat (tumblehome), however, the mold must be split down the middle. In this case, the initial layers of the laminate are usually laid up on each mold section, the two parts of the mold bolted together, and the two halves of the hull joined by lapping progressively wider layers of reinforcing material along the centerline joint. When the molds have been removed, there will be a crevice down the center line on the outside where the joint was formed; this area is filled with polyester putty and, if done well, is not noticeable.

Sometimes, also, part of the deep keel or skeg assembly of a sailboat is laid up in a separate small mold because the area would otherwise be unreachable. After the skeg or keel section has been laid up, the small mold is bolted to its larger sister; the skeg or keel laminate is then wed to the hull by overlapping the hull lay-up into the smaller section. In addition, any boat that uses a hull flange which turns in toward the center of the boat to make the hull–deck joint also requires a multipart mold. Mold strips for the flange must be attached along the top of the hull mold so that the flange can be made an integral part of the normal lay-up. Those mold strips must be removed before the hull can be pulled. All of the extra labor to provide the inward flange, of course, adds cost to the boat.

CONVENTIONAL LAY-UP METHODS

Three basic steps are involved in the production of fiber-reinforced plastic boat hulls from a female mold: (1) preparation of the mold, (2) application of the gel coat, and (3) application of the reinforcing fibers, or laminates. There is little practical difference from builder to builder in the first two steps. There may be great differences from one builder to the next in the third step; however, all of those differences have their basis in one of three methods for putting down the reinforcing fibers and building the laminate: 100 percent chopper gun, 100 percent hand lay-up, and a mixture of chop and hand lay-up. No one of these approaches, of course, is necessarily best in all circumstances. Each method has advantages and disadvantages. Each also requires use of good work practices to ensure a good product.

Mold Preparation

Molds are prepared by ensuring their cleanliness and by applying a so-called mold release agent, a waxlike substance that keeps the gel coat of the new hull from sticking to the mold. For complex molds, it may be necessary to apply a new coat of mold release agent before each use of the mold; with some very simple hull molds, however, it may be possible to pull as many as 15 hulls from the mold before applying a new coat of the mold release agent.

Gel Coat Application

The gel coat is applied with a spray gun that mixes the MEK peroxide initiator with the gel coat resin. Color pigments usually have been added to the resin by the resin manufacturer. The gel coat resin is fogged onto the mold surface, much as paint is sprayed onto a car or boat. Unlike a spray paint job, however, which often involves applying two separate coats of paint, a boat's gel coat is applied all in one operation. Generally, builders try to obtain a gel coat thickness of about 20 mils (20 thousandths of an inch). Though it is a quality control step too often overlooked, gel coat thickness can be tested during construction by the use of a wet mil gauge. The gel coat should be sprayed slightly thicker than the 20 mils desired to allow for shrinkage during the curing stage. By close monitoring of wet film thickness, a skilled operator can apply a very consistent coat. If too thin, the gel coat will not provide adequate protection for the laminate; if too thick, it will be vulnerable to cracking and crazing.

Before the first layers of reinforcing fibers are applied to the mold, the gel coat resin is allowed to cure to the desired degree of hardness. Although not commonly done, this hardness can be measured using a spring-loaded device with a sharp pin that is pushed into the gel coat. The device measures the pressure required to push the pin a given distance into the gel coat. As the resin cures, more force is required to push the pin into the gel coat. Depending upon the resin system, a hardness reading in the upper 30s or low 40s on one commonly used system, the Barcol scale, indicates that the gel coat resin is sufficiently cured to receive the subsequent layers of the laminate.

Laminate Application

A typical hull laminate has two basic parts: One is the so-called "skin coat," which is applied directly to the gel coat resin; the second is called the backup laminate and consists of the subsequent layers of the lamination (Fig. 3). The skin coat gen-

—————— Gel coat

▓▓▓▓▓▓ Chopped strand mat

ıﬂıılııııııııı Woven roving

Fɪɢ. 3.   Anatomy of a solid fiber glass laminate.

erally consists of one or more layers of chopped fiber totaling from ¾ of an ounce to 3 ounces per square foot and serves two functions: The smooth, homogeneous surface of the chopped fibers, whether in mat form or sprayed on with the chopper gun, helps ensure a uniform void-free and strong bond between the gel coat and the laminate structure; equally important from a marketing viewpoint, the skin coat helps prevent the pattern of subsequent layers of woven reinforcement from showing through the gel coat and creating a waffle appearance. Although this so-called pattern show-through is of no concern from a structural viewpoint, it is generally considered unattractive. In addition, some builders believe the skin coat is key to preventing blistering of the gel coat below the waterline, a problem that has plagued fiber glass boat owners and builders for years. According to this view, application of a resin-rich skin coat will prevent such gel coat blistering.

The subsequent layers of the laminate may consist either of all chopped fiber or of alternating layers of chopped fiber and a continuous strand fabric such as woven or unidirectional roving. In the case of chopped fiber, the fiber glass reinforcement can be applied by hand or with a chopper gun; continuous strand fabrics such as woven roving must be applied by hand.

Chopper Gun

The chopper gun has been much maligned and stoutly defended as a boat building tool. The focus of the argument is over the quality of laminates produced using the gun. From a practical perspective, the arguments boil down to two factors: the skill of the person using the chopper gun and the suitability of the application. Regardless of the merits on either side of the argument, the fact is that many builders use chopper guns in laying up their hulls. Some use the chopper gun exclusively; others use both the gun and hand lay-up. Some also use the chopper gun well; others may not.

According to the experts at Owens Corning, many boat hulls up to about 20 feet in length and some even larger are built using only chopped roving applied with a chopper gun. The argument for chop is generally made on costs:

It uses the least expensive form of fiber glass—continuous strand roving delivered on large spools.

It has the lowest glass content in the finished lay-up, about 26 to 27 percent by weight in a reasonably good job. Insofar as resin is cheaper than fiber glass, the low glass (high resin) content helps keep down costs.

It is generally the fastest way to apply reinforcing fibers.

It minimizes the labor content of the laminating procedure, particularly in building smaller boats.

In sum, the chopper gun provides the most economical way available for laying up fiber glass reinforcing fibers and resin in a hull mold within this size range.

However, 100 percent chop also has disadvantages, most of which relate to strength and weight. The lower glass content of the laminate means it will not be as strong as a laminate with a higher glass content. Moreover, because there are no long fibers in the reinforcement, the laminate will have a comparatively low resistance to impact damage and to fatigue from flexing. Usually builders compensate for these lower-strength factors by increasing the thickness of the laminate, but that in turn makes the boat heavier. The added weight may reduce the carrying capacity of the boat and make it necessary to use a larger engine or sail plan to obtain the desired performance under power or sail. The use of all chop may also make a difference in how well the boat holds up in service. One practical demonstration of these differences can be seen by comparing a Dyer dinghy that is several years old with an all-chop dinghy. Friends of ours have one of the early Dyer dinghyes and it remains in excellent condition after nearly 30 years of use. The thin, flexible hull of the Dyer is made using fiber glass boat cloth as the primary reinforcement. It is comparatively light in weight and has a remarkable carrying capacity. By contrast, the thick chop hull of our own dinghy, now just a few years old, has cracked beneath the center-line support for the midships thwart. The dinghy is heavy and its carrying capacity, despite the official rating, is limited to two adults in all but placid waters for fear of swamping. Of course, our dinghy cost less than half the price of the comparable-length Dyer.

Chop is applied in four intertwined steps. The operator first sprays a layer of resin onto the gel coat or previous layer of the laminate; the resin may be tinted so that the operator can see where it is sprayed and how much is laid down. He next turns on the chopper and sprays both chopped fibers and resin onto the mold, building up a loose fluffy layer of reinforcing fibers and resin. The operator can judge how much chop he has laid down and the evenness of application by watching the thickness and evenness of this fluffy layer.

The last step in applying the chop involves rolling down the fluffy layer of the fiber / resin mixture. This is done by workers using ridged aluminum rollers, working close behind the chopper gun operator as he moves down the mold. These special rollers (typically called "laminating rollers") are used to compact the fibers and to work the resin thoroughly through the laminate. As each layer is completed, the operator can come back for another pass, until the desired thickness of the laminate has been built up or the resin kicks off (gels). In this kind of operation, it is important that laminates not be made too thick too fast because of the heat given off as the resin cures. Workers also need good supervision; it is easier to roll out the chop if there is an excess of resin and unsupervised workers may therefore tend to use extra resin to make the job easier. The resulting laminate frequently winds up being resin rich and glass poor, the glass content dropping into the 20 to 25 percent range, according to one large builder who uses chopper guns extensively in his operations.

There are practical limitations to the chopper gun system, however. For example, although many boats up to about 20 feet in length are made of 100 percent chop, few boats of more than 25 feet are all chop. One reason is that as the boat size increases, it takes so long to cover the surface area using chop that the gun's advantage is lost. With smaller boats, by contrast, the speed of application lets a single crew spray up several hulls in the morning and their decks in the afternoon. The obvious result is a comparatively high level of productivity per unit of labor.

Hand Lay-up

Construction using all chop has one major limitation that simply cannot be overcome: Only short reinforcing fibers can be used in the laminate. None of the continuous strand fabrics with their far superior strength and performance properties can be used in the lay-up. If the design and use requirements of a boat demand use of woven roving or any other continuous strand fabric in the laminate, the builder is forced to turn, at least in part, to a hand lay-up system. Some builders opt for all hand lay-up, bypassing the chopper gun entirely.

Done properly, hand lay-up involves six steps, two more than required for the chopper gun: (1) The fabric is cut to size; (2) about a third of the resin to be used for any given laminate is sprayed onto the surface; (3) the fabric is laid into the mold. (4) If the fabric is mat, the remainder of the resin is sprayed before attempting to roll it out, because dry or partially wetted chopped strand mat tends to shed badly; if the fabric is a woven or uni-directional roving, normally it will be rolled out against the underlying laminate before the balance of the resin is sprayed onto the fabric. (5) The resin is worked into the fabric with rollers to ensure full saturation of the fabric. With heavier woven fabrics, special care is needed to be certain the resin is worked into the innermost fibers. In fact, the reason for applying a layer of resin before spreading the fabric is to allow resin to seep up from the underside as well as down from the top. Here, too, it is easier to roll out and wet out the reinforcement if there is an excess of resin; in short, good supervision is also needed for hand lay-up operations to avoid resin-rich laminates. (6) Excess resin is squeegeed from the laminate. Although this step is omitted in many lay-up shops, removing excess resin helps optimize the glass-to-resin ratio of the finished laminate. As noted earlier, this saves unnecessary weight.

In the hand lay-up method, the skin coat usually consists of one or more layers of 1.5-ounce mat. Subsequent laminates typically consist of alternating layers of woven roving and mat. When 24-ounce woven roving is used, 1.5-ounce mat is placed between plies of the woven fabric. When 18-ounce woven roving is used, ¾-ounce mat may be used. The mat is needed to provide a good mating surface between layers of the woven fabric. The under / over weave of the woven roving creates high and low spots on the fabric surface that make it difficult to obtain a good bond between layers if one ply of woven roving is put down directly on top of another.

The principal advantages of the hand lay-up system (Table 3) are that it enables builders to lay up moldings using long fibers as the primary reinforcement and to obtain higher glass-to-resin ratios than are possible using all chop. A hand lay-up also ensures a more uniform laminate thickness. As mentioned earlier, the glass-to-resin ratio in a laminate consisting of all

Table 3   Advantages of Different Lay-up Methods

Chopper gun	All hand lay-up	Hand lay-up and chop
Least expensive materials	Potentially highest strength (potentially high glass-to-resin ratio)	Good strength (potentially good glass-to-resin ratio)
Minimum labor content	Potentially high impact resistance (choice of reinforcing fabrics)	Potentially high impact resistance (choice of reinforcing fabrics; chop and mat a trade-off)
Speed of application for boats up to about 20 feet	Improved placement of reinforcement	Chop component reduces cost of materials and labor
	Potentially the longest useful life for the boat	

chop will be in the range of 26 to 27 percent. Typical glass-to-resin ratios from alternating layers of 24-ounce woven roving and 1.5-ounce mat are about 35 percent. With good technique, the woven roving / mat system may reach a glass content of 45 percent. With use of lighter weight woven roving and mat systems, for example, 18-ounce woven roving and ¾-ounce mat, slightly higher glass contents can be obtained. Disadvantages of hand lay-up include higher cost of materials and labor (Table 3A).

Chop Plus Hand Lay-up

A number of builders have combined the fabrication advantages of the chopper gun with the performance advantages of hand lay-up by using the chopper gun in place of handlaid mat.

Table 3A   Disadvantages of Different Lay-up Methods

Chopper gun	*All hand lay-up*	*Hand lay-up and chop*
Relatively heavy	Highest cost in materials	Increased potential for uneven application of reinforcement and resin in chop layers
Potential uneven quality in application.	Highest labor content	Somewhat lower than optimum glass-to-resin ratio
Relatively low strength (low glass-to-resin ratio)	More skilled labor required to maximize advantages	
Relatively low impact resistance (only short-fiber reinforcement)		
Shorter useful life for the boat		

In principal, it is difficult to see why such a marriage does not provide the best of both worlds. The chopper gun is used to put down the skin coat (Photo 9), which is then rolled out using the ridged aluminum rollers. Once the skin coat has cured adequately, resin is sprayed onto the laminate, woven roving spread out and squeegeed down, and more resin applied (Photo 10). When the woven roving has then been rolled out thoroughly by hand, another layer of chop is applied to provide the bonding surface required for the next layer of woven roving (Photo 11). In theory, this sytem should provide the same glass-to-resin ratio obtained by an all hand lay-up. In practice, however, because it is designed for efficiency and speed, it does not provide the same results. The layer of chop usually has a lower glass-to-resin ratio (about 26 or 27 percent) than an equivalent

9. A chopper gun is commonly used to lay up boats in the 25-foot and under range. Resin is fed from the barrel behind the worker, catalyst is supplied to the gun from a container attached to the barrel, and strands of roving are fed to the chopper gun from spools on the rack above the barrel. The stray line down the middle of the picture is a broken strand of roving hanging from the overhead boom.

10. After the skin coat and an added layer of chop have been applied, woven roving is spread out in the mold. The fabric has been cut to size before being brought to the laminating area.

11. As co-workers continue to lay out the woven roving, smoothing the wrinkles with flexible plastic paddles, a gun operator sprays resin onto the woven roving. The workers will then work the resin into the fabric using ridged metal rollers. (Photos by Susan Roberts)

layer of chopped strand mat (about 30 percent). Laminates of 24-ounce woven roving run about 45 percent glass. How can this information be helpful? It lets you evaluate builders' claims. For example, one builder of a popular production power boat whose hulls are laid up using both a chopper gun and hand lay-up, and who says he uses a resin-rich skin coat to help prevent blistering, claimed that the glass content of his hulls averages 57 percent. If his claim is accurate, the laminates clearly are starved for resin and one might think twice about buying his product.

LAY-UP SCHEDULES

The actual amount of reinforcing fiber that goes into a laminate may vary greatly from one boat to another, even among boats of similar size. As a result, it is not possible to use laminate thickness or a lay-up schedule alone to determine boat quality. The reason is as follows: From a structural viewpoint, the shell of a boat usually consists of two elements—the skin used to keep water on the outside and the framework used to help support that skin from the inside. In engineering the hull laminate, the laminate thickness and lay-up schedule are determined by the area between the stringers and frames used as interior reinforcing members, as well as the structural characteristics of the laminate itself. In general, if the spacing between interior reinforcing frames is larger, the laminate must be thicker. If the spacing is smaller, the laminate can be made thinner. The role of such interior reinforcement is discussed in greater detail in Chapter 6.

With that caveat about thickness and lay-up schedules understood, it is worthwhile looking at "typical" lay-up schedules. In general, larger boats tend to have more layers of reinforcement because they are subject to higher stresses. There are also differences in lay-up schedules for powerboats and sailboats because of the different stresses those hulls encounter. For example, a typical 20- to 25-foot planing powerboat intended for sport fishing may be built with the following lay-up schedule (Fig. 4):

FIG. 4.   Lay-up schedule for a typical 20- to 25-foot planing powerboat.

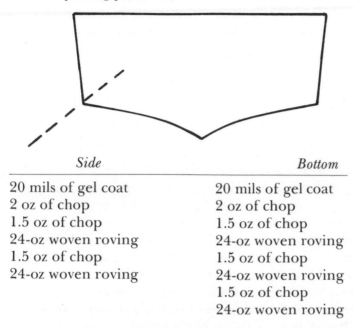

Side	*Bottom*
20 mils of gel coat	20 mils of gel coat
2 oz of chop	2 oz of chop
1.5 oz of chop	1.5 oz of chop
24-oz woven roving	24-oz woven roving
1.5 oz of chop	1.5 oz of chop
24-oz woven roving	24-oz woven roving
	1.5 oz of chop
	24-oz woven roving

In making a somewhat larger powerboat—up·to about 34 feet, for example—only one more layer of 24-ounce woven roving may be added, but additional chop may be used to beef up the stiffness of the laminate by making the hull thicker. For example, one 34-foot boat sold as a relatively slow-speed cruiser (12 knots crusing speed, 18 knots maximum) has a total of 18 ounces per square foot of chop (equivalent to 12 layers of 1.5-ounce mat) along with four layers of woven roving in the hull bottom. The builder commented, however, that they were studying the possibility of taking out some of that chop because they believe the hull is overbuilt.

According to data from Owens Corning, the laminate schedule above for the smaller powerboat, properly done, should result in a hull bottom thickness of about $5/16$ inch and a topside thickness of just under ¼ inch. The bottom of the 34-foot hull should be just over ¾ inch. If any of these laminates is resin rich, it may be up to 50 percent thicker, but it would also be more brittle. If a laminate has been thoroughly squeegeed to optimize the glass content, it might be as much as 25 percent thinner; it would also be lighter and stronger. In the case of the 34-foot boat, the builder commented that the hull thickness is just over 1 inch, about a third greater than what the Owens Corning data would lead one to expect.

The lay-up schedule for a sailboat hull may be more complex than that of an ordinary powerboat because of the different loadings. For example, the keel area usually needs extra ￢ein-forcement. Not only may the keel consist of several thousands of pounds of lead, but large sideways forces are placed on the keel structure both as the boat moves through the water and as it heels in response to the wind pressure on its sails. Similarly, the chain plate area may require extra reinforcement because of the loadings from the mast and shrouds, and the sides of the hull near the waterline may need stiffening because the boat sails on its side to some extent as it heels.

The lay-up schedule for one 35-foot sloop in the racer–cruiser category follows. As shown in Figure 5, the topsides extend from the shear to the waterline; the bottom extends from the water-line to the turn of the bilge into the keel. Note that the lay-up schedule for the transom is different from that for any of the other hull sections in that a layer of 1.5-ounce mat has been dropped before the first layer of woven roving—presumably to save weight in the stern.

Topside	Bottom
Gel coat	Gel coat
3-oz mat	3-oz mat
1.5-oz mat	1.5-oz mat
24-oz woven roving	24-oz woven roving
1.5-oz mat	1.5-oz mat
24-oz woven roving	24-oz woven roving
	1.5-oz mat
	24-oz woven roving

Keel	Transom
Gel coat	Gel coat
3-oz mat	3-oz mat
1.5-oz mat	24-oz woven roving
24-oz woven roving	1.5 oz mat
1.5-oz mat	24-oz woven roving
24-oz woven roving	1.5-oz mat
1.5-oz mat	24-oz woven roving
24-oz woven roving	
1.5-oz mat	
24-oz woven roving	

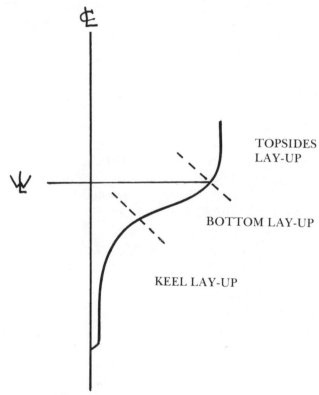

FIG. 5. Lay-up schedule for a 35-foot racer/cruiser sloop.

Where the fabrics in the topsides, bottom, and keel area meet, they overlap one another by 12 inches. In addition, two more layers of 1.5-ounce mat and two of 24-ounce woven roving are laid along the turn of the bilge into the keel as added reinforcement for the keel structure. The topside thickness of this laminate would run just over ¼ inch; the bottom thickness should be about ⅜ inch; the keel area should be almost ½ inch thick. The waterline and turn-of-the-bilge areas would be significantly thicker, of course, because of the 12-inch overlap of the reinforcing fabrics. The extra laminate at the turn of the bilge would make that area thicker still.

A 30-foot boat from the same builder intended more for racing shows still a different—and much lighter—lay-up schedule (Fig. 6). This boat has an external cast iron keel bolted to the hull. The keel reinforcement is laid down in an area about 4 feet wide and 8 feet long in the middle of the hull shell. The "belly band" is a strip about 18 inches wide that runs down one side of the hull, across the bottom, and up the other side in the area of the chain plate attachment and mast step. The lay-up schedule for the hull shell, which includes the topsides and bottom from one side to the other, is presented to show the order in which each layer of reinforcement fabric is applied. Note that the belly band is applied before the keel reinforcement and that the keel reinforcement is applied before the final two layers of the hull shell laminate.

Hull shell	*Belly band*	*Keel*
Gel coat		
1.5-oz mat		
1.5-oz mat		
18-oz woven roving		
	1.5-oz mat	
	18-oz woven roving	
		1.5-oz mat
		24-oz woven roving
1.5-oz mat		
18-oz woven roving		

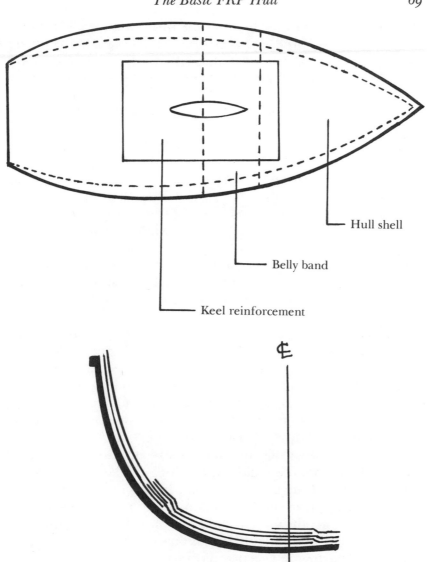

Hull shell

Belly band

Keel reinforcement

FIG. 6. (a) Placement of reinforcement in 30-foot sloop with an external lead fin keel. (b) Cross-sectional view illustrating overlap of reinforcing fabrics.

The lightest part of the laminate for this 30-foot sailboat is in the transom—also probably an effort to save weight in the stern. Additional stiffening is provided for the transom chain plate to carry the backstay loading.

Transom	Backstay stiffener
1.5-oz mat	
1.5-oz mat	
24-oz woven roving	
	1.5-oz mat
	24-oz woven roving

The hull shell of this boat would be less than ¼ inch thick; the keel area would be about $^5/_{16}$ inch thick. The transom would be just over ⅛ inch thick, except where it is beefed up for the backstay.

One question that may be asked, of course, is how long it takes to lay up these hulls. The 20- to 25-foot powerboat hull illustrated is produced in 24 hours from gel coat to removing the hull from the mold. At one plant, for example, several molds are prepared and the gel coat applied during the graveyard shift from 10 P.M. to 6 A.M. During the day shift, the skin coat and laminates are applied. During the next shift, reinforcing stringers (to be discussed in Chapter 6) are installed and the hull is pulled from the mold. A new hull can be started again that same night using the same mold. In this particular operation, the builder uses the DCPD laminating resins, which cure more rapidly than the more usual orthophthalic laminating resins. Product literature for DCPD laminating resins says clearly, "Good manufacturing practice dictates sanding between laminates." The reason for this recommendation is that DCPD resins cure rapidly and are based on a different chemical backbone. As a result, sanding is required to ensure a good bond between the laminates. In our visit to the builder whose production schedule is described above, we saw no effort made to sand between laminates.

Several days may be required to lay up the hulls for larger

boats. Normally, sanding would not be required between the laminates if general-purpose laminating resins are used—even if the hull sits overnight between laminates—because the general-purpose resins cure more slowly and are more forgiving. However, if the hull sits over a weekend between laminates, some builders recommend scuff-sanding the surface before applying the next laminate. The longer a laminate is allowed to cure before the next layer is applied, the less the styrene in the new layer of resin is able to penetrate the surface of the previous laminate to form cross-links between the resin surfaces. In addition, the longer the interval between laminates, the more likely the surface is to become dirty. Scuff sanding both cleans and roughens the surface, allowing a strong mechanical bond between the old and new layers of the laminate. Although there is no magic time limit after which every one agrees the laminate should be sanded before applying the next layer, there seems to be a consensus that sanding is advisable if as much as 72 hours has passed since the previous layer was applied.

VACUUM BAG MOLDING

Almost every junior high school science student learns about vacuums and air pressure. One common experiment involves pumping air from an otherwise empty can and watching the air pressure in the room crush the can as the vacuum within increases. Another involves placing an egg in the opening of a milk bottle, heating the bottle to drive off some of the air within, and then allowing both the bottle and the remaining air within it to cool, thus creating a partial vacuum until the surrounding air pressure pushes the egg into the bottle. This is the same atmospheric pressure that weathermen talk about when they speak of high-pressure and low-pressure areas flitting across the weather map. It is also the same atmospheric pressure that pushes against our eardrums, sometimes painfully, when we go down a long hill or are in an airplane descending from cruising altitude to a landing. This air pressure is basically the weight of all the air stacked up in the atmosphere over our heads wherever we are. At sea level, it amounts to about 14.7 pounds per square inch, or a bit over 1 ton per square foot (144 square inches).

Vacuum bagging is a system designed to make this normal atmospheric pressure work for us by using it to squeeze the resin in the laminate into the reinforcement fabrics (Fig. 7). After the reinforcement fabric has been laid up and the resin applied, a plastic film is placed over the mold and a vacuum drawn under the film. In essence, the plastic film and the exterior of the mold form the sides of the can from the science class experiment. As in the experiment, in which the air pressure

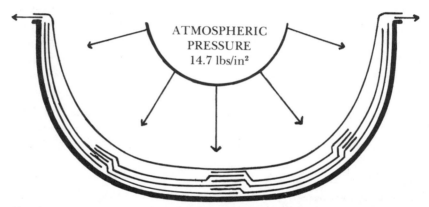

FIG. 7.   Vacuum bag system. The weight of the air in the atmosphere presses against the "vacuum bag," a plastic sheet covering the laminates, compressing the layers of reinforcing fabric tightly against the mold.

pushed against all sides of the can and crushed it, the atmospheric pressure pushes against the outside surfaces of the mold and plastic film covering the laminate from all directions, effectively crushing the plastic film tightly over the laminate. The force of the air pressure, potentially more than a ton per square foot, pushing the plastic film against the laminate squeezes the resin into the reinforcement with an efficiency far greater than workers using laminating rollers and squeegees can achieve. As a result, the reinforcement fabric is thoroughly saturated.

In wet lay-ups, the efficiency of the vacuum bag in saturating the reinforcement lets builders plan the glass-to-resin ratios ahead of time. They simply weigh the reinforcement, calculate how much resin is needed to obtain the desired glass-to-resin ratio, and then lay up the hull with confidence that the laminate will be fully saturated so long as the resin is distributed properly throughout the mold.

More recently, vacuum bag techniques have also been applied to molding systems using prepregs. In these so-called "dry layups," the vacuum bag system is used to compact the laminate and to help the resin flow once it has been heated to the required temperature. The application of vacuum bagging and prepregs to the production of relatively large structures was pioneered for the aircraft industry, where high strength and low weight are critical. The dry lay-up technology has been slow to catch on in the boating industry, however—probably for two reasons: Most boat owners do not demand the high performance potential offered by use of prepregs and vacuum bagging, and a sizable capital investment is required on the part of the builder to construct a mold capable of withstanding the 250°F temperature needed to cure the laminate, to build an oven large enough to contain the mold, and to provide refrigerated storage for the prepregs before they are put in the mold.

Although wet systems using vacuum bags do not require any particular capital investment, they too have not been widely used, both because of the system's inherent limitations and because of the difficulty in using it well. After the reinforcement fabrics have been laid into the mold (over the gel coat), the measured amounts of resin must be spread throughout the mold. This resin, of course, will tend to pool in the bottom of the mold while the vacuum bag is being applied and the vacuum is drawn. As a result, workers need to move the resin around after the vacuum has been drawn by squeegeeing it through the vacuum bag. All of this, of course, takes time. As a result, the gel time of the resin must be closely controlled to be certain gelation does not occur before the resin has been distributed evenly throughout the mold. An experienced crew is also helpful. In general, one would not attempt to build either a thick laminate or a large hull using the wet vacuum bag system because of the difficulty in applying the larger volume of resin evenly, and in moving it around after the vacuum has

been pulled to ensure an even distribution of resin—all before
the resin begins to gel. As a result, its use is generally limited to
lightweight and mostly small hulls. Because of these limitations,
the system is most likely to be used principally in small yards
for production of high-performance boats built on a quasicustom basis.

4

Composite Construction
Technology of the Future Today

For all of its assets, fiber glass has one key disadvantage as a boat building material: It is quite flexible; that is, it bends easily. At first blush, this flexibility might be considered an advantage in a hull: If the boat bumps into something, the hull will give with the impact. The potential problem, however, is one of fatigue. Any material that is flexed excessively on a continuing basis will become fatigued eventually and may fail. For example, bending a piece of wire back and forth is a time-honored way of breaking the wire if you do not have a pair of snips handy. Bending or "flexing" the wire excessively and repeatedly fatigues it until it breaks, or fails. In the same way, repeated, excessive flexing of a fiber glass panel—for example, a section of a hull—may eventually lead to failure. This means, of course, that a boat must be designed and constructed to provide sufficient stiffness and strength in the hull sections to prevent excessive flexing and protect overall structural integrity.

Traditionally, builders have solved the flexibility problem in two ways: First, they have used internal floor members, stringers, bulkheads, and furnishings as a framework to reinforce the hull. Powerboat builders, for example, have generally made

extensive use of framework in the bottom of their boats to reinforce the flat planing surfaces against the heavy, repeated
pounding a boat absorbs as it slams from wave to wave at planing speed. Sailboats, of course, are subject to different stresses.
As a result, builders have been able to rely more on interior
bulkheads and furniture to reinforce their hulls, particularly
against stresses from the rigging and against the repeated wave
impacts topsides as a boat beats to windward, heeled over by
the wind. (The use of interior components to strengthen the
hull will be described in more detail in Chapter 6.)

The second method for stiffening hull sections has been simply piling on the layers of fiber glass materials to make the hull
thicker. The role of thickness in overcoming the flexibility of
fiber glass can be illustrated by using two pieces of lumber. If a
20-foot board 1 inch thick is placed across two sawhorses, one
at each end, the board will sag in the middle (Fig. 8). If another
20-foot board—this one 4 inches thick—is placed across the same
two sawhorses, it certainly will not sag as much and it probably
will not sag at all because the surfaces of the board are farther
apart and the wood fibers must stretch further to allow the board
to sag. The thicker board will, however, weigh four times as
much as the first one.

Adding thickness to fiber glass panels has the same two effects:
It adds stiffness and weight. It also adds strength because of
the added layers of reinforcing fabric. Some builders, of course,
have gone to extremes with hull thickness, particularly in the

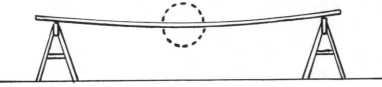

FIG. 8.   A 20-foot long board placed across two sawhorses may sag
a bit between the two supports. While the overall bending is visible
to our eyes, the amount of bend in any one short section of the
board is so slight that the individual surface fibers along the bottom
of the board do not have to stretch significantly. If enough weight
were put on the center of the board, however, it would bend until
the surface fibers were stretched beyond their capability and the
board would break across the bottom.

sailboat industry in the mid- to late-1970s, when hull thickness was often made an ultimate virtue. For example, Westsail touted its thick laminates loudly in promoting the strength of its boats. Similarly, CSY focused an important part of its sales promotion on the thickness of its solid fiber glass hulls and decks, comparing the thickness of core samples from its boats to those of another boat whose hull sections were considerably lighter in construction. (Both Westsail and the CSY boat building company are out of business today.) Along with that hull strength, however, both Westsail and CSY boats paid a heavy penalty in added weight.

"Too much weight" is the overriding problem posed by thick fiber glass laminates. Among powerboats, more weight means either slower speed, bigger engines, or both. It also means higher fuel consumption. Among displacement sailboats, more weight for a given waterline length means either poorer sailing performance in light and moderate winds or the need for larger sails, larger winches, and heavier standing and running rigging to compensate for the heavier displacement. Among both sailboats and powerboats, more weight often means also heavier anchors, chain, and lines. Among both powerboats and sailboats, more weight may mean more cost to build as well.

In the past few years, the demand for improved performance in both powerboats and sailboats has led many builders to seek different solutions to the problem of the flexibility of fiber glass. Their goal was to save weight. A number of approaches have been used. Some builders have simply looked at the numbers, decided that their hulls have been overbuilt all along, and removed one or more laminates from the lay-up schedule. In the sailboat industry, finally recognizing that the size of the unreinforced hull section is more important in determining hull thickness than the size of the hull itself, some builders have reduced the number of laminates and beefed up the hull by using more involved stringer and frame systems in the bilges—systems similar to those used in powerboats for years. Hull liners (to be discussed along with stringer systems in Chapter 6) represent still another approach to the problem. In high-performance boats, builders have begun turning to unidirectional roving and to reinforcements made of S-glass and / or

Kevlar. Increasingly, however, in both powerboats and sailboats, builders are turning to some kind of composite or "sandwich" type of construction in which part of the laminate is
replaced by a lightweight core material. In the process, these
builders are not merely trimming off unneeded pounds; they
are often building stronger hulls as well.

Composite construction, of course, is not new to the boating
industry. Plywood cores have been used to strengthen decks for
years. Countless boats also had their transoms reinforced with
plywood. The difference is that builders today are turning in
large numbers to the use of composites in the hulls of their
boats. In fact, the use of composites has played a key role in the
extension of fiber-reinforced plastic (FRP) construction to larger
boats—80-foot motor yachts, commercial fishing trawlers of
about the same length, and now government patrol boats of
even larger sizes.

In general, high-volume production boat builders do not turn
to composite construction to save money. Although use of a
core usually allows a builder to reduce the amount of mat, woven
roving, and resin in his hull lay-up, the core itself costs money
and requires at least the same labor (some builders say up to
one and a half times the labor) required to lay up a layer of mat
and woven roving.

Under some circumstances, however, the use of a core may
reduce costs. In large boats, for example, where several layers
of mat and roving can be dropped from the laminate schedule,
the savings in reinforcing materials, resin, and labor may be
great enough to outweigh the cost of the core materials. In
medium-sized boats, the relatively low cost of balsa core (compared to other core materials) also may offer some cost savings
compared to a solid FRP hull.

Cost considerations aside, the principal attraction of composite construction is the high strength-to-weight ratio it offers. In
addition, composite construction generally provides insulation
against temperature, sound, and vibration. As a result, the cool
weather and cold water sweating problem characteristic of solid
FRP lay-ups is often eliminated. Moreover, composite construction usually makes heating (or air-conditioning) a boat easier.
It may also result in the boat running more quietly and with
less vibration.

Although the core material contributes to the overall strength of the composite, the two surface layers of any panel carry the major loads, not the middle. In a very thin panel, such as a thin laminate of solid FRP, the two surfaces are so close together as to be essentially one. As a result, that thin panel will bend easily. In a composite construction, the core's principal function is to hold the two fiber glass skins a fixed distance apart so that they cannot "act as one." For the panel to bend significantly, one skin must either stretch (which it won't) or the other must compress (which it won't). This increases the stiffness or "strength" of the panel. In a perfect world, before the panel would bend, one skin and half the core would tear and the other skin and remainder of the core would bend. This is the way, for example, a green (not dried out) piece of wood like a tree branch breaks.

Looking again at the inch-thick board considered earlier to see the practical effect of composite construction, it turns out that this 20-foot board is actually two ½-inch pieces of wood that have been fastened together to make up the 1-inch thickness. Of course, it still sags badly when placed across two sawhorses. However, if we separate the two ½-inch layers, put a 3-inch-thick plank between them, and fasten the three layers together, we have made an all-wood "composite" that has two ½-inch "skins" and a 3-inch core—a total thickness of 4 inches. This composite structure will perform just like the 4-inch board used in the earlier example: It will not sag between the saw horses. It will, however, weigh just as much as the single 4-inch thick board. We could accomplish the same strengthening effect another way as well: by putting a 3-inch-thick foam or balsa core between the two ½-inch wood "skins" and then fastening the sandwich together with a strong adhesive. This composite structure also would perform just like the 4-inch board used in the first example; it would not sag between the saw horses. It would, however, weigh considerably less than either the all-wood "composite" or the original 4-inch-thick solid board.

Putting a wood or foam core between two fiber glass skins has the same effect. For example, a hull made with an end-grain balsa core is 9 to 10 times stronger than an identical hull made using the same fiber glass laminate, but without the balsa core in the middle. This tremendous increase in strength from use of the core gives boat designers much more freedom in design than a solid FRP hull laminate offers. For example, the increased stiffness of the cored laminate structure means the hull does not need as much interior reinforcing to prevent flexing. As a result, designers can open up interior arrangements. It also means they can design for better performance because of the weight-saving opportunities offered by the composite construction. For example, by designing a cored hull to provide the same strength as an existing solid FRP hull, it is possible to reduce the boat's weight by up to 50 percent. The opportunity to save weight, of course, increases with boat size.

Let us look at three boats built using cored hulls. At one end of the spectrum, Huckins builds the hull of its 80-foot motor yacht using Airex foam with a total of barely over ½ inch of fiber glass in the topsides and just over ⅝ inch in the bottom. With two layers of ¾-inch Airex foam between the inner and outer fiber glass skins, however, the total hull thickness is more than 2 inches. If it were built in solid fiber glass, the same hull probably would average about ¾ inch in thickness, requiring about three more layers of 24-ounce woven roving and 1.5-ounce mat. The hull would also probably require substantially more interior framing and definitely would weigh more. The extra laminates alone would add about 2.25 pounds for every square foot of hull surface. As you can imagine, when you add up the surface areas of the bottom, sides, and transom of an 80-foot motor yacht's hull, that's a lot of added weight. Moreover, that total would not include the weight of additional interior framing needed to stiffen the solid fiber glass hull.

At the other end of the spectrum, one can look at the J-24, a fast, one-design sailboat whose performance and quality made it an almost instant commercial success. The J-24, which has a relatively flat bottom for a displacement sailboat, is constructed of ⅛-inch fiber glass skins over a ⅜-inch balsa core. The boat is light enough to plane easily, and the hull panels are stiff enough that they hold their shape even under these severe stresses— one key to the boat's outstanding performance. The J-24 reportedly has hit speeds up to 15 knots—flying for a 24-foot monohull sailboat. Without the core, the hull's flat bottom panels would need added interior reinforcement and more glass in the

FIG. 9. Cutaway view shows the lay-up of a balsa-cored composite.
The bottom of the section represents the outer skin.

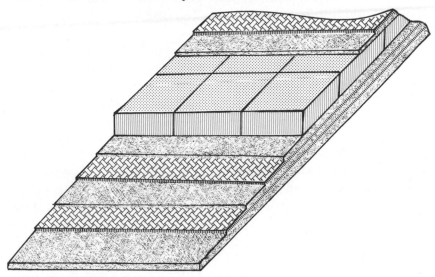

laminate. Both would mean more weight, and the exciting performance of the design would be lost.

Gulfstar's 39-foot Sailmaster falls somewhere in the middle
of those two extremes. The balsa core is carried from the shear
to within about 2 feet of the center line of the hull. The laminate schedule calls for an outer skin just over ¼ inch thick and
an inner skin about ⅛ inch thick (Fig. 9). The lay-up schedule
for that hull is as follows:

> Gel coat
> 1.5 oz of chop
> 1.5-oz mat
> 24-oz woven roving
> 1.5-oz mat
> 24-oz woven roving
> 1-oz mat
> Balsa core
> 1.5-oz mat
> 24-oz woven roving
> 1.5-oz mat

Two additional layers of 24-ounce woven roving and 1.5-ounce mat are used wherever there is no balsa core. Gulfstar estimates that it would add between 10 and 15 percent to the cost of the hull to build it in solid fiber glass.

From a consumer's perspective, of course, the field of composites in the boating industry resembles an obstacle course in which the object is to negotiate a mishmash of claims and counterclaims made for the various core materials. Balsa is said to be the strongest; balsa is said to suffer from water problems. Airex is said to be best because it is flexible; Airex is said to have problems with high temperatures. Klegecell is said to be stronger than Airex, and lighter than balsa; Klegecell is said to be weaker than balsa and to fail catastrophically, whereas Airex will give and recover. This is just a sample of some of the claims. The facts are these:

• Each of these core materials is a good product.

• Each has certain characteristics that make it attractive to one builder, but perhaps less attractive to another, or more attractive than another core for specific applications.

• Each of these core materials is being promoted by sales and advertising people trying to convince you and me that their product is best.

• Each boat builder using these core materials tries to justify his decision by focusing on the apparent advantages of his choice and the disadvantage of other products.

• Thousands of boat hulls ranging in size from dinghy to more than 140 feet in length have been built using end-grain balsa, Airex foam, and Klegecell foam. Thousands more—but a smaller number—have been built using other core materials in at least part of the hull.

• There are three keys to the effective use of these products: (1) that no material be used for a purpose it is not suited for, (2) that the boat be designed around whatever materials are used, and (3) that correct procedures be followed in building the composite.

The point is this: All of these products have been used well and successfully. There are differences between them, but the engineering that goes into their use in a specific boat is more important than the relative properties of the materials themselves, advertising claims notwithstanding (Table 4).

Table 4   Key Properties of FRP Construction Methods[a]

Airex foam	*Balsa*	*Klegecell foam*	*Nomex honeycomb*	*Coremat*	*Solid FRP laminate*
Relatively low stiffness	Very high stiffness	Good stiffness	Ultralightweight	Replaces mat layer saving weight of mat; no resin savings	Very heavy for comparable stiffness and strength
High impact resistance	Lightweight	Lightweight	Exceptional strength	Increases panel stiffness, but does not increase strength	Low stiffness; requires thick layup or more frequent interior framing
High cost	Low cost	Relatively low shear strength	Costly, relatively complex technology	Easy application, low cost	Relatively easy to work with
				Low shear strength	

[a]NOTE: Differences in stiffness and shear strength must be taken into account in the design of the laminate and interior reinforcement.

END-GRAIN BALSA

Today's end-grain balsa core is produced by taking a balsa tree, slicing it much like you would slice a salami, and then laying those slices out to make the core. The problem, of course, is that boat hulls are generally curved and that ½- or ¾-inch-thick slices of balsa tree trunk will not bend to fit those curves. To get around this, the slices of balsa are cut into a series of small rectangles or squares and laid out on a lightweight polyester fabric (scrim) resembling an extralight cheesecloth. The scrim is glued to the balsa to hold all of the little pieces together. When it is finished, a sheet of the core looks a bit like a large, floppy jigsaw puzzle in which all of the pieces are squares or rectangles. As you look down on this puzzle, there is no picture, of course, but you are looking at the ends of the wood grain in each little puzzle piece—hence the name "end-grain balsa" (Photo 12).

Installing the core material is somewhat more complex than laying up a fiber glass laminate. In general, builders estimate about 25 percent more labor is needed to lay in a single layer of balsa core than to apply a laminate of 24-ounce woven roving and 1.5-ounce mat. After laying up the outer skin, a resin-rich (80 percent resin) layer of 1.5-ounce mat or chop is put down

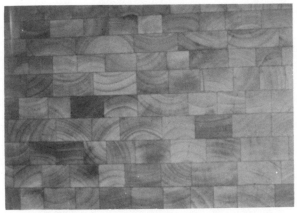

12. End-grain balsa core, with the different rings and coloration of each block creating a checkerboard or jigsaw puzzle effect. (Photo courtesy of Baltek Corporation)

as a bedding layer for the core. If the core is wet out before being laid into the bedding layer, the resin used to wet the core should be included in calculating the 80 percent resin-to-glass ratio of the bedding. The sheets of end-grain balsa are then laid down on this wet layer of mat and pressed against the laminate by hand until resin oozes up between the squares of balsa. Generally, the core is laid down right after the wet mat has been rolled out. After the bedding layer has cured, adhesion of the core to the outer skin can be tested by tapping it; wherever the core has pulled away from the skin so that there is a void, the tapping will result in a hollow sound. Such spots can be marked and repaired before putting down the inner skin. The importance of applying the core to the outer skin properly cannot be overstated. The most difficult part of applying any core material is ensuring a good bond between the outer skin and the core; you cannot see through the core to be certain there are no voids—air spaces—in the bond. Such voids, which could later act as conduits for water, will form wherever the core is not held tightly against the outer skin until the bonding resin has set up.

Wherever the core ends, it should be beveled so that the inner skin can be brought smoothly down to join the outer skin at the core's edge (Fig. 10). This beveling can be done by sanding the

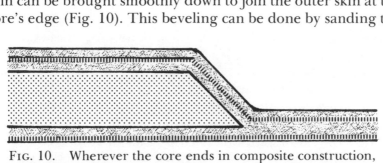

FIG. 10.   Wherever the core ends in composite construction, either the core itself should be beveled or a fillet should be placed along the edge of the core so that the inner FRP skin is brought down gradually to join the outer skin to avoid creating a stress (hard) spot at the core edge.

core, applying a fillet (a wedge-shaped filler), or using a polyester putty to form the beveled edge. After sanding and filling any gaps in the core, a minimum layer of ¾-ounce mat or chop is applied to begin laying up the inner skin. Because the balsa does soak up some resin, it is useful to wet out the core before applying the layer of mat or chop.

End-grain balsa is the most widely used core material in boat construction. Although it is the strongest core material by a wide margin, the factor contributing most to its popularity is probably its comparatively low cost. End-grain balsa is only about three-quarters the cost of Klegecell and three-fifths that of Airex on an equal thickness basis. On an equal strength basis, the relative cost of balsa is even lower, because thicker cores of Airex and Klegecell are required to achieve the same strength offered by the balsa, if one assumes the same laminate schedule. The low cost of end-grain balsa provides another incentive to boat builders as well. It alone among the three major core materials may offer builders an opportunity to cut costs by changing to composite construction.

Along with its low cost, balsa carries some other attractions from the builder's point of view. It is easier to work with than most other core materials; the balsa is available in a wider range of thicknesses than are competitive foam core materials; and it is lighter than Airex and about the same weight as the medium-density Klegecell foam most commonly used in the boating industry. In addition, there is the comfort factor: A lot of other production boat builders have used and are using balsa successfully; this fact makes it easier to create new converts.

Balsa, however, carries two liabilities for builders: one easily dealt with, the other more difficult to overcome. The easily solved problem involves pattern print-through. The pattern of the small pieces of balsa that make up the core may show through the outer skin unless care is taken to prevent it, for example, by using a thicker skin coat than might otherwise be necessary. The more difficult problem is a marketing problem: overcoming possible consumer concern growing out of horror stories (most exaggerated) about damage to hull structure from water getting into the core. Because these stories abound, some builders will not use any balsa core below the waterline; some will not use it anywhere in the hull—or perhaps in sailboats, but not in powerboats. There is little logic to these decisions from an engineering viewpoint; usually, in fact, these are marketing decisions, not engineering decisions.

Although concern about potential water damage to balsa core materials has its foundation in experience, that experience occurred years ago with a totally different product than is used today. About 20 years ago, some builders used balsa planks to core the hulls of their small runabouts. In a plank, of course, the grain of the wood runs along the length of the board. If water gets into the plank anywhere along its length, the grain of the balsa wood will wick water along the entire length of the plank. If there is enough water over a period of time, the affected plank will be turned to mush as the water progresses. Unfortunately, that is exactly what happened to some of those boats when the FRP skin was broken and water penetrated into one or more of the balsa planks. Some builders wound up repairing those boats for several years. It should be noted also, however, that some of those boats are still in service today.

Although that experience could not be repeated using today's end-grain balsa core materials if good lay-up procedures are followed, the fact that it did happen once has been enough to plant seeds of doubt in some minds. But consider the facts: The grain in those planks 20 years ago ran the length of the hull and helped spread the water; the grain in today's balsa cores runs through the thickness of the hull and works against the spread of any water.

This claim for balsa core is not mere puffery. Lloyd's Register of Shipping has run tests that back up the assertion that water will not migrate through a properly installed end-grain balsa core. As a result, Lloyds has accepted end-grain balsa construction for certification since the mid-1970s. It is worth noting, however, that Lloyd's emphasizes it will accept end-grain balsa core for certification only if the core is "applied under close supervision of the Society's Surveyors," a standard Lloyd's practice, but noteworthy all the same because of the importance of proper installation. It is also worth noting that good practice dictates removing the balsa core around any through-hull fittings. Even if water would not spread from a leak around a fitting, the core in the immediate area of the leak would be softened by the water and would need repair.

PVC FOAMS

Next to end-grain balsa, the most widely used core materials for boat hulls are closed cell PVC (polyvinyl chloride) foams. There are two of these products, best known in the United States as Airex and Klegecell foam. Both also are sold widely outside the United States; they were invented and developed in Europe, although the licensing arrangements for the Klegecell-type foam result in its being produced under the trademarks Divinycell in Sweden and Plasticell in the United Kingdom. Some 30,000 boats have been built around the world over the past 30 years using the Klegecell-type core materials in some portion of the boat; another 20,000 have been built using Airex. Although the two products are classed generically as PVC foams, they are distinctly different from each other both in chemical structure and in performance characteristics. Moreover, they compete strongly with each other as well as with end-grain balsa to gain market share in the boat industry. However, they have to compete with balsa on some basis other than cost, because neither PVC foam product promises builders significant cost savings in what are normally considered production boats, for example, under 50 feet. In fact, the marketing manager for Airex says flatly, "No one ever chooses Airex to reduce costs."

The foam core materials are produced in solid sheets and in contoured sheets made up of 1½-inch squares that will flex to fit the contours of a hull. The contoured sheets of Klegecell are held together by a lightweight fiber glass scrim. The Airex contour sheets are somewhat different. When the sheets are cut into the 1½-inch squares, the knife leaves small, uncut sections connecting the individual squares to hold the sheet together.

In general, the lay-up procedure for both Klegecell and Airex contoured foams, is similar to the procedure used for end-grain balsa. There are, however, subtle differences of which builders need to be aware. This means that someone who is accustomed to using end-grain balsa cannot just assume he would follow identical procedures for these foams and be assured of doing a good job. For example, Klegecell is best used with resins having a slightly faster gel time than is recommended for balsa core; Airex, on the other hand, should be applied using a longer gel time than is recommended for balsa. As another example, it is generally recommended that both foams be wet out before being laid into the bedding layer, whereas wetting out the balsa core is considered optional, possibly because the foams do not have balsa's natural tendency to "soak up" resin. Still another example is that tapping the foams will not tell much about the continuity of the core-to-skin bond; however, scraping the foam lightly with a coin will reveal any voids in the bond, also by a change in the sound.

Klegecell

Klegecell is a mixture of PVC and polyurethane-type compounds characterized chemically by cross-linking that yields a strong, rigid, but somewhat brittle foam. A key attraction of Klegecell foam is its light weight—only half the weight of end-grain balsa and a fourth that of Airex foam. In comparison to an FRP / balsa composite, this weight advantage of Klegecell is increased because the end-grain balsa core soaks up resin, therefore requiring more resin in the laminate to achieve a good bond between the core and the FRP skins. The additional resin adds weight to the panel. At the same time, composites made using Klegecell foam are relatively strong. Laboratory tests indicate that FRP / Klegecell composites are somewhat more than half as strong as comparable end-grain balsa composites, and 30 to 40 percent stronger than comparable Airex cored panels. What this all adds up to is this: Composite panels made with Klegecell provide the highest strength-to-weight ratio available using conventional core materials.

Airex

Airex is a semirigid thermoplastic foam produced from pure PVC compounds. In contrast to the relatively brittle cross-linked chemical structure of the Klegecell-type foam, Airex is characterized by the absence of any cross-linking. As a result, Airex foam will bend and can be compressed. For example, at room temperature, a ⅜-inch thick piece of Airex can be bent (slowly) to a U shape around a 1-inch-thick bar without breaking. Similarly, the foam can be squeezed (compressed) down to half its normal thickness without rupturing the bubbles (cells) that make up the foam or crumbling the cell walls. Upon release, the foam will slowly regain its original shape.

Because it is flexible and can be compressed, composites made with an Airex core tend to be more resistant to damage from impact than those using either end-grain balsa or Klegecell foam. The Airex cored panel is also more resistant to impact damage than a solid FRP laminate. The reason is that both the panel and the Airex core itself give a bit with the impact, absorbing and spreading the energy. Although the outer skin may be damaged, the inner skin is protected by the energy-absorbing characteristic of the Airex core. In contrast, end-grain balsa transmits the impact directly from the outer skin to the inner skin. The Klegecell foam absorbs some of the impact energy, but the effect is mostly just to spread it out a bit in transmitting the force of the impact to the inner skin. The solid FRP laminate tends to perform similarly to the balsa cored panel; the impact energy is transmitted directly through the laminate.

The flexibility of the Airex core has important implications for boat builders. For example, an Airex composite is only about two-thirds as strong as a similar composite made with Klegecell foam. And then it will bend. The reason for this, as noted earlier, is that a composite panel cannot bend significantly without either stretching (or tearing) one skin or compressing (or buckling) the other skin *so long as the two skins are held a fixed distance apart.* When sufficient bending force is applied to the Airex panel, the core will "give," or compress, allowing the inner skin to bend more than the outer skin (Fig. 11). In effect, the two

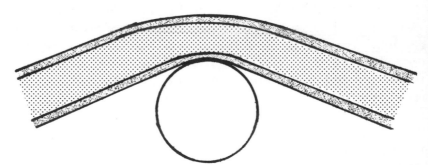

FIG. 11. The flexibility of Airex foam lets the core be compressed under a bending stress so that the inner and outer skins can bend somewhat independently. While this characteristic contributes to the superior impact resistance of Airex composites, it also explains why composites made of Airex have lower bending strength than composites made using either end-grain balsa or Klegecell foam, assuming all three are made using the same lay-up schedule.

FIG. 12. In balsa and foam-core composites, builders should remove the core material and bring the inner and outer skins together wherever deck fittings and through-hull fittings are placed. This protects a balsa core from possible water damage should the fitting installation leak. It protects a foam core from being crushed (Klegecell) or compressed (Airex) when the fasteners are tightened and from putting unwanted stresses on the laminate structure.

skins now are bending somewhat independently, and the whole panel bends as a result. (This characteristic is in contrast to the performances of Klegecell and end-grain balsa, both of which, though stronger initially, tend to fail suddenly if they are over-stressed.) From a practical viewpoint, this means builders must compensate for the flexibility of the Airex core by using either a thicker core, thicker skins, more closely spaced stringers and frame members, or some combination of the three. As a result, of course, the potential weight savings from using the Airex core is lessened. Similarly, the ease with which the Airex core can be compressed means builders should either use spacers or remove the core wherever fittings or bolts are put through the hull (Fig. 12). Without such precautions, a worker can easily compress the core when tightening down on a bolt, creating an unwanted stress point in the hull structure. In addition, the flexibility of the Airex hull means that all interior components must be bonded securely to the hull to help provide stiffness to the hull sections, as is the case with solid FRP laminates. Hulls cored with Klegecell foam and balsa are considerably stiffer in their own right and so do not rely to the same extent on interior bulkheads and furnishings for structural integrity.

Other PVC Foams

A few builders may also use low-grade open-cell PVC foams in nonstructural areas to increase panel thickness and stiffness.

However, because of their open-cell structure, such foams will soak up water like a sponge if water gets to them. For that reason, the use of an open-cell foam as a core material is questionable anywhere in a hull. Its use is also questionable anywhere else in a boat where a leak around a fitting or fastener (screw or bolt) may provide a pathway for water into the core.

CLOSED-CELL POLYURETHANE FOAM

Polyurethane foam is generally not recommended today as a core material for composite construction in the marine industry because it is considered by many to be too "friable"; that is, it has a tendency to crumble. One builder, however, has proved a very successful exception to that rule. All of the Boston Whaler single-hull boats have been made using a closed-cell polyurethane foam between two hull shells. The Whaler system involves laying up the outer and inner hull shells separately, mating them, and then injecting the foam into the space between the two shells. The foam expands to fill the space and adheres tightly to the two hull shells, forming a unified structure.

COREMAT

Builders who do not want to use a composite construction but who do want to reduce the hull weight of their boats may turn to a product called Coremat. As the name suggests, this product includes elements of both a core material for composite construction and the chopped strand mat used in most fiber glass laminates. It represents, in short, a compromise between use of a foam or balsa core and a solid fiber glass lay-up.

Coremat is neither fish nor fowl as a boat building material. It has no structural performance characteristics of its own— core shear strength, stiffness, compression strength, and so on— as do balsa and PVC foam core materials. Nor does it provide any structural reinforcement to the laminate as do the fiber glass materials it replaces. It does, however, add bulk—thickness—at about one-half the weight of the fiber glass laminates it replaces.

By adding thickness, of course, the Coremat adds stiffness to the panel.

The key to Coremat is microballoons—tiny particles of dust to the naked eye, but hollow plastic spheres under a microscope. These microballoons weigh almost nothing but take up a lot of space. Coremat essentially provides an easy way of applying a layer of microballoons between the layers of reinforcing fabrics to increase the thickness of the laminate. These microballons are carried in a nonwoven polyester fabric held together by an acrylic binder that is dissolved by the styrene in the polyester resins. By itself, the Coremat material resembles a soft, white felt. It is covered with perforations at about half-inch intervals to assist in resin penetration. When properly wet out, the Coremat layer consists of 50 percent microballoons and 50 percent resin. Each perforation in the Coremat fabric is filled with hardened resin, contributing to the compression resistance of the core. The weight saved is mostly that of the fiber glass material the Coremat has replaced. Some additional weight may also be saved, because slightly less resin is used with the Coremat than with an equivalent thickness of fiber glass fabric. Coremat is available in thicknesses from 1 to 5 millimeters, 5 millimeters being slightly less than ¼ inch.

The principal attractions of Coremat are the opportunity to either save weight with no increase in labor by substituting the Coremat for one or more layers of glass fabric, or increase layup thickness (and therefore its stiffness) without the added labor required for other core materials. The Coremat goes down just like a layer of chopped strand fiber glass mat, requiring only good laminating procedures to ensure good resin saturation. Although the cost of Coremat is slightly greater than that of the fiber glass materials it replaces, the small resin savings is said to balance out the materials cost. As a result, use of Coremat is said to be cost competitive with a solid fiber glass laminate in laminates of between ⅛ and ⅝ inch in thickness.

As with most compromises, however, Coremat has limitations. For example, engineers we spoke with do not recommend trying to build up a thick core with the material because it has a low shear strength, relying as it does upon the resin for its structural properties. As a result, thick layers of Coremat will fail under load much sooner than balsa, Airex, or Klegecell. One engineer notes, for example, that although his company has had good success using the 4 millimeter (slightly less that $^3/_{16}$ inch) Coremat in the hull of a 40-foot sailboat, they have had problems in trying to use two 4-millimeter layers to core a deck.

Such factors limit the amount of hull stiffening and weight savings possible using Coremat on larger boats, where use of other thicker and stronger core materials may save two or more layers of both woven roving and chopped strand mat and improve rather than compromise the structural properties of the hull. In smaller boats, however, the limitations may be less. One builder, for example, says his company has had good results using a 2 millimeter layer of Coremat in the sides of powerboat hulls in the 25-foot range in lieu of a laminate of 24-ounce woven roving and 1.5-ounces of chop. Use of Coremat in this application saves the builder about 26 pounds in hull weight and about $26 in costs. Although the cost savings is not much when considered on the basis of an individual boat, the company's volume of hundreds of boats per year makes that small savings significant on an annual basis. It should be noted, however, that if the Coremat is used to replace fiber glass reinforcing fabric on a one-to-one basis in an effort to save weight, the builder may significantly reduce the structural properties—particularly the impact resistance—of the laminate. Most builders we spoke with who use Coremat recommend it either as a supplement to the skin coat to prevent pattern print-through or as a lighter-weight alternative to extra layers of FRP to stiffen areas where the structural limitations of the material are not important. Such applications include hull liners, the deck of some boats, and such nonstructural interior components as the walls of a shower stall.

NOMEX HONEYCOMB

In years past, paper honeycomb structures have not had a good reputation in the boating industry. Although theoretically honeycomb composites have offered the greatest possible increase in strength at the lowest possible weight, the kraft paper honeycomb suffered two key shortcomings: It presented problems of water migration if one of the skins was broken or punctured and it lost most of its strength when it got wet. As a result, honeycomb was labeled.

Nomex honeycomb is slowly rewriting that "label." Not only is water migration through the new honeycomb essentially "zero," but also honeycomb made of Nomex paper retains about 80 percent of its strength even when wet. Moreover, by now enough boats or parts of boats have been built using this new honeycomb material that more builders are now starting to take a second look at honeycomb technology. The reasons are the following:

• As a rule, it is possible to save from 30 to 50 percent of the weight of a given component by using honeycomb and fiber glass composite in place of solid fiber glass; more weight savings is possible by combining the honeycomb with such materials as Kevlar.

• The honeycomb is extremely strong and stiff, so that hulls can be built as a monocoque structure requiring few interior bulkheads; as a result, the entire interior is usable space.

• The honeycomb provides inherent floatation. Builders of the Stilletto catamaran claim their hulls will float even if filled entirely with water, because 90 percent of the volume of the composite is air trapped in the honeycomb structure.

Nomex itself is an aramid fiber that, in this case, has been made into a paperlike material. That paper is then made into the honeycomb structure and impregnated with a phenolic resin to make the paper stiffer and to increase its water resistance (Photo 13). The honeycomb core is most easily used with prepregs and a vacuum bag system. It is not difficult to imagine the potential problems in a wet lay-up caused by resin running into the honeycomb cells. The core easily could be filled with resin in places, and the reinforcing fabric starved for resin as a result. Such problems can be avoided, however, through a process in which the builder essentially makes his own "prepregs" as he is laying up the boat. The method requires using a thickened epoxy resin system and wetting out the fabric shortly before it is applied. In some systems, the resin may be allowed to cure partially before the wet-out fabric is applied to the honeycomb. In others, the resin may be thick enough that the fabric can be put directly onto the honeycomb after wetting out. The cure can be allowed to take place at room temperature, although an oven is often used.

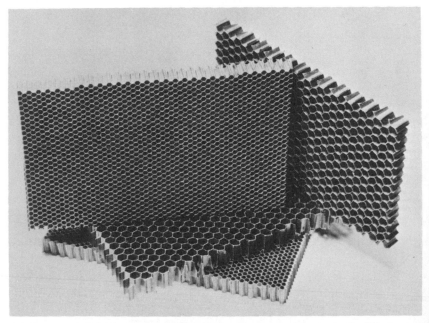

13. Honeycomb core material of Nomex aramid paper is fabricated with different hole sizes in the honeycomb structure and is cut in different thicknesses, depending upon the structural requirements of the laminate. (Photo courtesy of Du Pont Company)

Except for the need to use a vacuum bag system, prepregs simplify the use of a honeycomb core. The dry (waxy to the touch) preimpregnated reinforcing fabric can be laid into the mold to form the outer skin, the honeycomb put in its place, and one or more additional prepreg layers put on top of the honeycomb to form the inner skin. After the vacuum bag has been installed and a vacuum drawn to squeeze the prepregs and honeycomb down tight against the mold, the entire structure, including the mold, is wheeled into an oven and baked to effect the cure.

One factor that contributes to the exceptional strength of the FRP / honeycomb composite is the natural tendency of the pre-preg resins to form a meniscus in each cell of the honeycomb. We see other examples of a meniscus virtually every time we take a drink from a glass. By holding the glass up so that we are looking across the surface of the water, we can see that the water forms a small arc where it meets the glass, climbing the side of the glass $1/16$ of an inch or so. That curvature of the water surface as it meets the sides of the glass is the meniscus. Similar curves of resin are formed along the edges of every cell in the honeycomb as the oven heat turns the dry resin of the prepregs into a liquid. As that resin cures, each meniscus hardens too, providing a strong bond between the skins and the honeycomb (Fig. 13).

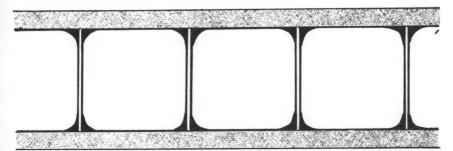

FIG. 13.   A cross-sectional illustration of a honeycomb compos-ite illustrates how the resin climbs the honeycomb wall to form a natural "fillet" bond between the core and the two FRP skins.

The attraction of the honeycomb composite is its extremely high strength-to-weight ratio. For example, a composite struc-ture made of fiber glass and honeycomb materials has nine times the resistance to bending of stainless steel on an equal weight basis. From a practical perspective, that means designers can build great strength into their boats with large weight savings. Alternatively, they can carve weight from their boats by using honeycomb composites for components. For example, one builder offers a special package for his 53-foot boat that takes advantage of honeycomb composites to carve 2,000 pounds from the boat's overall weight. Other examples are as follow: Force engineering has shown one powerboat builder a honeycomb engine hatch that weighs only 11 pounds instead of the standard hatch's 38 pounds. Similarly, Force built a sunshade for a trawler that saved the builder 650 pounds. The sunshade measured 14 by 16 feet and had to be strong enough to support five adults. The standard structure weighed 800 pounds. The honeycomb structure weighed 150 pounds, and it easily supported the five people.

But there is a catch. The materials and technology of honeycomb composites are expensive. For example, a honeycomb composite for a bulkhead costs 8 to 10 times as much as a plywood bulkhead. Although some people are willing to pay that added expense to save weight, most are not. Nor, when the market opportunity is so limited, are most production boat builders yet willing to make the capital investment required to install a vacuum bag system, oven, and refrigerated storage facilities for prepreg materials, and to build the new, high-temperature molds needed for this system.

5

Custom Hulls
From Inside Out

Using a female mold to build FRP boats is practical only when the builder expects to sell a substantial number of boats made from that mold. But what about the custom boat builder? Or the small yard that wants to build a few boats from one design, but not enough to justify the expense of a female mold? Or even the production boat builder who wants to build a fiber glass plug from which to make a female mold? In the earliest years of fiber glass boat construction, the answer to these questions was a boat built with wood, and then fiber-glassed. Today, drawing upon modern technology, custom builders generally pursue one of three basic approaches to completing the hull. One approach has grown out of composite construction using an Airex or Klegecell foam core. Another is based on the C-flex system for building a solid FRP laminate. The third alternative—not commonly considered FRP technology—uses the WEST system of cold-molded wood construction.

All three of these systems for custom or "one-off" construction have a common denominator that reaches beyond the materials of construction. The hulls are built up over a framework that resembles the ribs and stringers of conventional wood boat construction. In certain cases, the framework may also have a "skin," usually of either Masonite or thin and inexpensive two-ply plywood. In the case of composite construction, this framework is temporary, serving only as a "male" mold. In both the C-flex system and the WEST system of cold-molded wood construction, the framework may also include bulkheads or stringers that will become part of the finished boat. The principal function of the frame, however, remains that of a male mold.

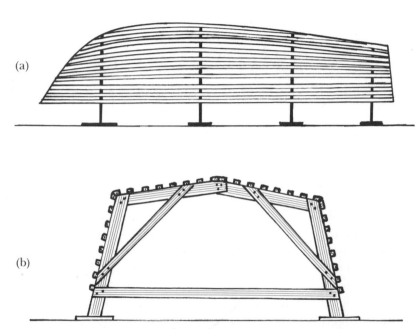

(a)

(b)

FIG. 14.   (a) A typical male mold is built using wood strips resembling stringers placed across a series of frames. The spacing between the wood strips varies, depending upon the type of construction to be used. (b) Cross-sectional view illustrates the placement of stringers on frames for a male mold.

All three systems share one other characteristic as well: When a production hull comes out of the female mold, the outer surface is already fair; its gel coat is shiny, the surface smooth, and very little cosmetic work is needed to finish off the hull surface. Not so for a custom boat. In this kind of construction, the hull is built up over the mold from the inside out. As a result, the gel coat is the last layer applied to the outer surface of the hull and will highlight any irregularities in the laminate surface. As a result, custom boats require a great deal of work after the actual construction of the hull has been completed to provide the kind of exterior surface finish boat owners have come to expect from FRP materials.

CUSTOM HULLS USING COMPOSITE CONSTRUCTION

To build a custom hull with fiber glass fabric and polyester resin, a builder needs a solid surface to support the first layers of the laminate. Without such a surface—for example, if the woven roving were simply stretched across an open framework—much of the resin would simply run through the fabric and drip onto the ground; in addition, the fiber glass fabric would sag badly around the frames. In short, it would not work. In the past, when builders put fiber glass over wood hulls, the wood planking or plywood sheathing provided the backup surface needed to hold the fabric and resin in place until the resin was cured.

Today one of two approaches is taken. The conventional approach involves "planking" the framework of the male mold with 18- by 36-inch sheets of Airex or Klegecell foam core and then applying the FRP laminates to the core. The newer approach, catching on in the United States at a relatively few custom yards only recently, involves putting an inexpensive "skin" over the framework of the male mold and laying up the hull from the inside out—exactly the reverse of the female mold system. In either instance, the result is a custom hull essentially identical in construction and performance characteristics to a production hull made in a female mold using the same core system. It consists of an outer skin, usually a foam or balsa core, and an inner skin. The major difference is the route by which each hull came into being.

"Conventional" Cored One-off Construction

Builders have been producing custom hulls for some years now using solid sheets of Airex and Klegecell PVC foams fit over male molds made using frame and stringer systems (Fig. 14). End-grain balsa and sheets of foam cut into small squares to make them flexible have generally not been used because the conventional male mold system did not provide the support needed to obtain a smooth surface finish.

Airex and Klegecell, of course, have different characteristics and there are some differences in how they are used to build custom hulls using conventional technology. One example is that in constructing the frame for the male mold, the battens or "stringers" are generally spaced 2 to 3 inches apart for Airex, but 3 to 6 inches apart for Klegecell. The reason for this is that the flexibility of Airex requires the closer spacing to avoid possible low spots caused by the foam settling between the stringers; or, as seen from the other point of view, the greater stiffness of Klegecell makes it possible to space the battens further apart. Despite such differences in detail, the basic steps in building a custom hull using the two foams are much the same.

If we look at the job of fitting a series of 18- by 36-inch rectangles of rigid or semirigid foam to the compound curves of a boat hull, it is readily apparent that the sheets of foam will not fit up against one another perfectly. For this reason, builders usually cover the wood framework with plastic sheeting to keep any resin that comes through cracks between the pieces of foam from "gluing" the core to the wooden framework.

The actual task of fitting sheets of foam core to the wood framework involves heating the foam to make it bend to the contours of the hull. It may also be necessary to leave gaps that can be filled in later by cutting pieces of foam to fit those "holes." The foam is usually attached temporarily to the framework in one of four methods:

• Nailing the foam to the battens with finishing nails. Once the FRP outer skin has been applied, the nails are pulled on through the foam from beneath the frame so that the hull can be lifted from the mold.

• Nailing the foam temporarily and then using screws from underneath the battens to hold the foam in place during the laminating procedure. The nails are removed before the lay-up begins. The screws are removed after the outer FRP skin has been completed.

• Using staples that will simply be pulled through the foam when the hull is lifted from the frame.

• "Stitching" the foam to the battens by running yarn through the foam and looping it around the battens. Such stitches can be cut before the hull is removed from the mold.

Before the first layer of fiber glass material is put over the foam core, two additional steps are necessary. Wherever the hull will have solid fiber glass sections (i.e., no core), blocks of wood the same thickness as the foam must be inserted in lieu of foam. Such areas might include the keel area, along the shear, or where chain plates bolt to the hull. Often these blocks of wood are built onto the frame itself. In any case, such wood inserts are coated with a mold release agent (or covered with waxed paper) so that the fiber glass resin will not adhere to them. When the hull is lifted from the mold, those blocks will be removed, the edges of the foam feathered, and the inner fiber glass skin brought down from the foam core to form a solid laminate with the outer skin.

The second step before applying any fiber glass material is fairing the foam. This involves filling any cracks with polyester putty and sanding the surface to do away with high spots. Time spent at this point and between subsequent layers of the FRP laminations making the surface as fair as possible will make the final finishing work much easier.

When the lay-up begins, the first layer of mat normally is resin rich to ensure a good bond between the foam core and the FRP skin. Recommended procedure involves wetting down the foam core with resin before laying out a minimum 1-ounce layer of mat. Once that first layer of mat has cured, successive layers of reinforcing fabrics are put down using normal good laminating practices, with one exception: The edges of each piece of reinforcing fabric are not overlapped as is usual practice; instead, they are butted up against one another. These fabric joints then are staggered in each new layer of fabric to guard against creating a weak spot in the laminate. Overlaps are avoided to prevent high spots that will later have to be faired out.

When the final layer of mat has been applied, but before the gel coat has been sprayed, the hull surface is carefully faired. After gel coat application, additional fairing using a polyester putty is often necessary to build up low spots revealed by the shiny gel coat. Usually, after all work to fair the hull is completed, the topsides are sprayed with a two-part polyurethane coating (see Chapter 9).

With the outer skin completed, the next step is to build a cradle to receive the hull after it is lifted from the male mold. After any screws or stitching used to fasten the foam core to the framework of the male mold are removed, the hull is lifted from the mold, turned over, and placed in its cradle. To prepare the hull to receive its inner skin, the builder bevels the edges of the foam core wherever the inner skin will be brought down to join the outer skin. Any spaces between the pieces of foam are filled using a polyester putty, and joints between pieces of foam are sanded to provide an even surface to receive the inner skin. Once the laminating begins, the builder follows the same procedures used when working with a female mold: prewetting the foam core, first applying a resin-rich layer of mat, and then applying subsequent layers of the lamination, overlapping the pieces of reinforcing fabric as in normal practice and adding extra laminates as scheduled for solid FRP areas.

The "New" Technology for Cored One-off Hulls

The addition of an inexpensive "skin" to the male mold lets custom builders reduce their costs in building a custom hull by 10 to 15 percent compared to more conventional cored construction technology. It should be noted also that, unlike the conventional system just described, use of the "skinned" male mold is not limited to use with foam cores. The addition of an inexpensive skin to the male mold enables builders to produce one-offs using either solid FRP laminates or virtually any core material. Also, when using foam core, the flexible sheets that have been cut into small squares can be used to ease the job of fitting the core to the curves of the hull. As with any such advance, however, there are trade-offs. The principal trade-off in this case is the need to use a vacuum bag system to ensure a good bond between the core and the inner skin.

When a "skinned" male mold is used, the lay-up process is similar to that used in building production boats in a female mold. First, a mold release agent is applied to the mold surface.

A light gel coat layer is sometimes applied; this layer of gel coat, of course, will cover the inner surface of the hull. The next step is application of the inner skin, which is allowed to cure and is then carefully faired before the core is applied. In principal, core application in this system is similar to the procedure described in Chapter 4. The back of the core is coated with resin and the core is then pressed into a resin-rich layer of mat so that excess resin is squeezed through the cracks between each small square of the core. In one-off construction, however, a vacuum bag system is generally used to press the core against the layer of mat and hold it in place until the resin has cured. Normally, because of the short working time with the polyester resin, only relatively small areas of core are applied at a time, the vacuum drawn, and the resin allowed to cure before moving to the next section. When the entire core has been applied, the builder can fair the core surface carefully before applying the outer skin. The relative ease of fairing the core to eliminate all surface irregularities before applying the outer skin compared to the difficulty of fairing the finished laminate provides opportunity for significant savings in labor.

There are two other principal areas of cost saving possible from this newer technology. In conventional one-off construction, the cradle constructed to receive the half-completed hull must be relatively elaborate. That hull, which is removed from the mold after the outer skin but before the inner skin has been applied, is very wobbly and must be carefully supported to ensure the desired shape. In contrast, the cradle for a hull built using the new technology can be less elaborate because the panel stiffness provided by the completed composite construction helps ensure hull shape. Another area of possible cost savings may be found in the relative ease of doing all of the work from outside the hull, rather than doing half the work from outside and the other half from inside after the hull has been placed in its cradle.

THE C-FLEX SYSTEM

The C-flex system is a relative newcomer to fiber glass technology. It was developed by Seeman Fiberglass, Inc., in the early

1970s as a means for building custom hulls using solid FRP lay-ups. The system combines the traditional concept of planking a hull with modern fiber glass technology. It has been used to build boats ranging in size and style from canoes to 40-foot rac-ing sailboats and to an 84-foot pilot boat. C-Flex itself is essen-tially a 12-inch-wide fiber glass "plank" made up of solid FRP rods running the length of the plank. Unidirectional fiber glass roving fills in the spaces between the rods and a lightweight fiber glass cloth ties the "plank" together until resin can be applied. C-Flex comes in 250-foot rolls and the "planks" are cut to length as needed. In general, a single "plank" runs the entire length of the hull. In fact, short "planks" of C-flex should not be placed end to end to make a longer "plank." Although a ⅛-inch-thick C-flex is used for most boat construction, a lighter product about $1/12$ inch thick is available for lightweight racing boats and canoes. The FRP rods—similar to thin sections of a fiber glass fishing rod—are spaced on about ½-inch centers across the width of the "plank." Although the solid FRP rods are flexible and will bend to take the compound curves of a boat hull, they contribute significantly to the stiffness of the finished laminate along the length of the hull.

Construction using the C-flex system does not require as elaborate a male mold as other methods of custom FRP con-struction. The solid FRP rods of the C-flex plank eliminate the need for longitudinal stringers or battens in the mold to sup-port the building materials between frame pieces. As in the case of the foam core method, however, the mold surfaces are cov-ered with waxed paper or coated with some other release agent to prevent the polyester resin from gluing the mold to the hull.

The C-flex planks are stapled to the frames, usually begin-ning with the keel and working toward the sheer. After the planks have been stapled in place, a polyester marble "casting" resin—as opposed to a standard laminating resin—is applied to the C-flex. The casting resin is recommended because it is char-acterized by very low shrinkage. If a standard laminating resin is used, resin shrinkage as it cures may pull the C-flex planks down tight between the frames, creating flat spots between frames rather than the intended gentle curves. Use of a "cast-ing" resin prevents this problem. The resin also is catalyzed to gel slowly so that there will be enough time for the resin to soak into the thick C-flex material before it gels. It is often necessary to apply additional resin as it soaks into the unidirectional roving between the solid FRP rods. It is also frequently necessary to apply additional resin to the C-flex planks from the inside of the hull after it has been turned over because the material could not be thoroughly saturated from the outside. The rods that form the backbone of the C-flex planks make "working" the resin into the fabric difficult.

Once the C-flex has been saturated with the casting resin, the hull is sanded lightly and a layer of each mat and woven roving are applied to the hull. Essentially all of the reinforcing strength of the C-flex planks, of course, is oriented along the length of the boat with the fiber glass rods. To provide greater strength from keel to shear, the woven roving generally is run athwartship rather than longitudinally, with substantial overlap along the center line of the keel. As each laminate of mat and woven roving is laid up, it is squeegeed with a wide steel putty knife to remove excess resin and air bubbles in the lay-up. This also helps fill in the grooves between the rods in the C-flex, thereby helping fair the hull as the laminate is built up. In light lay-ups, adjoining pieces of reinforcing fabric often are overlapped to ensure adequate panel strength. In heavier laminates, however, butting the edges of adjacent pieces of reinforcing fabric will help eliminate high spots. However, such butt joints in the fabric are staggered throughout the laminate.

The final mat layer on the outer surface acts as a fairing surface for sanding down high spots. Once the sanding is completed, a final coat of resin seals glass fiber ends that have been bared in the sanding. As in other one-off construction, a polyester putty is used to build up low spots. According to the manufacturer of C-flex, a good "commercial" finish will require about 1 man-hour of labor fairing the hull for each 10 square feet of hull surface, about 60 man-hours of labor for a light displacement 35-foot sailboat. A finish suitable for use as a plug for making a female mold would require more than five times as much work; others suggest that time spent fairing the hull will be even longer.

When the outer surface has been completed, the hull is lifted from the mold. The staples used to hold the C-flex to the planks will pull away from the mold with the hull. After the inside of the hull has been coated with resin wherever needed to finish saturating the C-flex planks, the protruding staple ends and any other burrs are ground off using a disk sander and the inside laminates are applied. Even in the lightest structure, a minimum of one layer of mat is required to provide adequate reinforcement on the inside of the hull, since all of the fibers in the C-flex plank run lengthwise. In most boats, layers of both mat and woven roving are recommended, and there may be several laminates. As on the outer laminates, the woven roving is run from the center line to the shear, with substantial overlap along the center line.

THE WEST SYSTEM OF COLD-MOLDED WOOD CONSTRUCTION

It does not require much stretch of the imagination to include the WEST system—wood epoxy saturation technique—as a form of FRP construction. Wood is, after all, a fibrous material. Epoxies are one of the basic resin forms used to build reinforced plastic structures, and, interestingly enough, tests have shown that WEST saturation can increase the stiffness and strength properties of wood.

The WEST system, developed, nurtured, and popularized by the Gougeon Brothers Boat Yard in Bay City, Michigan, begins with three basic concepts: (1) The less moisture there is in wood, the stronger the wood will be; (2) if wood can be kept at a constant moisture content, problems of drying out, shrinking, swelling, and weight gain by water absorption will be eliminated; and (3) if wood can be kept below 20 percent moisture content and sealed from the air, it will remain free of dry rot. The obvious common element is control of the moisture content of the wood.

The "green" wood of a freshly cut tree has a high moisture content. In essence, the hollow fibers that form the wood are filled with water; even the walls of these fibers are saturated with moisture. In time, of course, the wood dries until all of the water has evaporated from within the hollow fibers. At this point, the moisture content of the log has dropped to about 25 percent and the only water left in the wood is the moisture absorbed in the fiber walls. This condition of dryness is called the "fiber saturation point" of the wood. This is the condition of the bottom planking in conventional wood boats while the boat is in the water. If much drying occurs beyond this point—because the boat is hauled and kept in winter storage, for example—the wood is likely to shrink significantly (actual shrinkage varies with wood type). Ironically, as this drying occurs, the wood also increases in strength, and, as the moisture content of the wood drops below 20 percent, it also becomes too dry for dry rot to occur. When the boat is put back into the water, the moisture content of the wood goes back up near the fiber saturation point, the strength of the wood is reduced, and the dampness required for dry rot may once again exist.

One key to the moisture content of wood is relative humidity. Depending upon the relative humidity of the air around the wood, it can be dried naturally down to 10 or 12 percent moisture content. Of course, kiln drying can be used to dry the wood as well, but if the pieces of lumber come out of the kiln into a high-humidity environment, it will not be too many days before the wood has soaked up enough moisture from the air to bring it back near the fiber saturation point. The tendency of wood to absorb moisture from the air creates the need for either naturally occurring low humidity (as in the upper Midwest, where Gougeon Brothers, Inc., is located) or good mechanical humidity control to keep the moisture content of the wood low until the wood grain can be sealed off from the moisture in the air.

The WEST system developed by Gougeon Brothers uses epoxy resin to control the moisture content of wood used in building the boat hull. A specially formulated epoxy resin seals all of the wood's surfaces completely so that it cannot absorb moisture or dry out; in other words, once sealed in this manner, the moisture content of the wood remains what it was at the time the resin was applied. In this way, the builder can seal the wood when its physical properties are near their maximum (low moisture content), can prevent swelling of the wood when the boat goes into the water, and can eliminate problems of dry rot. He can also produce a "wood" boat that will not gain weight from soaking up water after being launched.

The WEST system tends to be used in one of two ways: first is the use of epoxy resin principally as a wood sealant in conventional strip plank construction; the other is the use of epoxy resin as both a sealer and an adhesive in the cold molding method of wood boat construction. It is this latter application that most closely resembles FRP construction.

In essence, cold molding uses thin (typically ⅛ inch thick) laminates of wood as a unidirectional roving. The grain of each laminate is oriented differently than it is in the laminate that preceded it. Moreover, frequently the hull is finished with one or more layers of fiber glass boat cloth below the waterline to provide abrasion resistance against possible accidental groundings or even intentional beachings. For example, a half-ton keel sailboat hull might be built using six layers of ⅛-inch veneer and a single layer of 6-ounce fiber glass boat cloth on the bottom for abrasion resistance. In ultralight hulls used for racing, unidirectional rovings of carbon fiber or S-glass are often used to strengthen the hull by forming stringers or ribs. For example, 1-inch-wide tapes containing as many as 40,000 continuous filaments of carbon fiber can be laminated one atop the other, running from keel to shear, to form a riblike structure to stiffen the hull section. Both carbon fiber and S-glass are also used to reinforce specific high-stress sections of the hull, such as chain plates, centerboard trunks, winch bases, mast steps, and rudder shafts.

Like the other systems for one-off FRP construction, the WEST system requires construction of a male mold, with longitudinal battens at closely spaced intervals to form the hull shape. Although most of the frames and battens are temporary, builders frequently prefabricate bulkheads, floor members, and reinforcing stringers to insert them into the mold so that the resin-sealed wood laminates are built up directly onto these structural members. In this way, the hull is stiffened considerably before it is lifted from the mold.

Once the framework has been completed and all reinforcing members placed within the structure of the mold, the inside of the veneer strips for the first wood laminate are prefinished with three coats of epoxy resin. As the first laminate is applied to the framework—usually at an angle of 45 degrees to the transversal and longitudinal axes of the hull—the mating surfaces of any bulkheads, stringers, and other reinforcing members are coated liberally with epoxy resin. The veneer is stapled to the frames and, as each new strip of veneer is put down, resin is applied to the mating edges of the wood.

When the first laminate has been completed and the resin has cured, the veneer surface is sanded thoroughly to provide a smooth mating surface for the next laminate. The second layer usually is applied at a 90-degree angle to the first laminate, with liberal coatings of the epoxy resin applied to both the outer surface of the first veneer and the inner surface of the second as the new strips are stapled in place. Edge gluing is not necessary after the first laminate, because subsequent coatings of resin will fill the joints between the strips of veneer.

The process continues—sanding each new veneer surface to provide a smooth mating surface for the next layer, coating the surface liberally with resin, changing the orientation of the next layer of veneer (probably orienting the veneer strips in the third layer lengthwise along the hull)—until the desired number of laminates has been laid up. A minimum of three coatings of resin is recommended for the outer surface. In addition, since epoxies are degraded by the ultraviolet light, the surface is protected from sunlight by a pigmented coating of epoxy, paint, varnish, or a two-part polyurethane coating. Of the four, the pigmented epoxy coating is least desirable; although the pigment helps protect the epoxy from the sunlight, the surface will become chalky. If any laminates of fiber glass cloth are planned to protect the hull bottom from abrasion, they usually are applied before the hull is removed from the mold.

6

Interior Components
A Source of Inner Strength

At a small yard in Sarasota, Florida, two people lay up the basic hull of an Airex-cored Vancouver 36 sailboat in about 7 working days. On the first day, the gel coat and two skin-coat layers of ¾-ounce chopped strand mat are applied to the mold. On the second day, a laminate of ¾-ounce mat and 18-ounce woven roving is put down. During the third day, two additional laminates of ¾-ounce mat and 18-ounce woven roving are applied. The fourth day brings the Airex core—laid down into a resin-rich layer of 1.5-ounce mat. On the fifth day, the inner skin is applied: a layer of ¾-ounce mat against the foam core followed by two laminates of ¾-ounce mat and 18-ounce woven roving. In the final 2 days, five additional laminates of ¾-ounce mat and 18-ounce woven roving are added from the turn of the bilge where the core ends down to the keel bottom where the laminations from each side overlap.

Then the real work begins—about 6 months of work, in fact, for four skilled workers to take that completed hull and turn it into a finished boat. Part of that time, of course, involves laying up the deck and fitting it out, and fitting a rub rail to the hull, fabricating and installing the rudder, and installing the ballast and engine. Most of that time, however, is spent putting in the interior, one piece at a time in what is essentially custom construction. It is the way interiors of boats have been put together for many years. The advent of "production" boats, however, has been changing this way of building boat interiors. The reason should be apparent: Time costs money. When builders review plant operations in the never-ending search for ways to cut costs, one obvious place to look is the part of the boat that takes longest time to complete—the interior.

Much progress has been made in recent years in controlling these costs, particularly in adapting assembly line techniques to boat building and standardizing components. In one large builder's plant, for example, work begins on the interior of a 25-foot sailboat 2 weeks before hull lay-up begins. Many of the wooden parts are cut by semiautomatic saws guided by patterns. The wiring harness has been designed for the boat and is prefabricated by an outside supplier. As smaller components are assembled, they are put together in a jig until the entire interior is prefabricated, ready to be dropped into the hull as a complete unit. This assembly line approach is used in boats as large as 40 feet or more by some builders. Even with larger boats in which the interior is too large and too complex to be preassembled, subunits are prefabricated in the shop so that when the boat is ready for them, the subunits are ready for installation in the boat.

One obstacle, however, keeps standing in the way of further efficiencies when building wood interiors: Most or all of the interior components should be tied into the hull in some manner. The reason is that in nearly all FRP construction, the interior should serve as an integral part of the boat's structural reinforcement. The situation is analogous to a key change that has taken place in automobile design over the past dozen years or so with adoption of unitized construction to eliminate the heavy frame pieces previously used for structural reinforcement. The shift from traditional wood boat construction to modern FRP technology represents the same kind of change.

The first components of an FRP boat's interior often are put into the hull before it has been removed from the mold. These may include stringers and frame systems designed to stiffen the large flat sections of hull bottoms and sides. In larger boats, key structural bulkheads also may be installed at this time. If not, at the very least temporary braces should be clamped from one side of the hull to the other. The reason for this is that an unreinforced FRP hull is surprisingly flexible and will wobble or sag out of shape easily. Installing stringers, frames, and bulkheads while the hull is still in the mold helps guarantee that the boat will retain the shape its designer intended for it even after it has been pulled from the confines of the mold. There is another advantage as well to installing reinforcing members early. Taking time to install key structural components "in the mold" helps ensure adequate cure time for the hull before it is put in a cradle. A hull that has been cradled at all carelessly while it is still green may become permanently misshapen.

STRINGERS AND FRAMES

Powerboats traditionally have required installation of complex stringer and frame systems to reinforce FRP hull sections against the constant pounding the boat bottom receives running through or over the waves. Though they are used principally in the hull bottoms, these reinforcing systems are analogous to the ribs and stringers used in wood boat construction. Until recently, the structural needs of sailboats have been somewhat different. The first reason, of course, is that sailboats generally move more slowly than powerboats and their hulls usually do not receive the heavy pounding that is often routine for powerboats. The second reason is that until recently sailboats usually have not had the large flat hull sections that characterize modern powerboats. The soft chines of fiber glass sailboat hulls and the traditional rounded turn of the bilge into the keel have generally made frame and stringer systems in the hull bottoms unnecessary. The curved shape of the hull itself and the interior components from the cabin sole up provided all of the panel stiffness that was needed. Today, however, designers seeking increased performance off the wind and stiffer rigs on the wind have turned to much flatter hull sections. In an effort to save weight in the hull, they have also trimmed lay-up schedules. In smaller boats, the use of such core materials as balsa and Klegecell foam in the hull has compensated to a large extent for these changes. In larger boats, however, the flatter hull sections and lighter lay-ups have brought about increased use of frame and stringer systems to strengthen these flatter, lighter hull bottoms. They have also brought about increased use of stringer systems above the waterline in forward sections of the hull to help distribute the loads as the boat sails heeled over, beating to windward.

The easiest illustration of such frame and stringer systems begins with a boat whose bottom starts out resembling a flat sheet of plywood. If we take three two-by-fours, cut them to size, and place them on their sides so that they run across the bottom of the boat, we have installed three frames (Fig. 15). If we then take two more two-by-fours, cut them to run the length of the boat, and notch them to fit over the frames, we have installed two stringers. The frames reinforce the bottom from

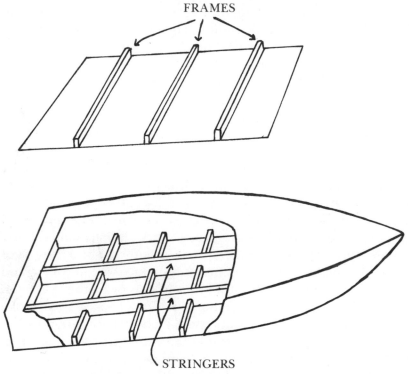

FIG. 15. Frames and stringers are used to reinforce the bottom of a boat. In the top illustration, three "frames" are placed across a sheet of plywood. In the bottom illustration, two "stringers" running along the length of the bottom have been added and the sheet of plywood converted into a boat bottom. Stringers also may serve as engine mounts, distributing the weight of the engine and the force of the propeller thrust throughout the hull structure.

one side to the other; the stringers strengthen it along the boat's length. Together the stringers and frames form a reinforcing grid or latticework. The design of this grid has important bearing on hull construction, particularly on laminate thickness and, therefore, overall weight. A hull with only small spaces between the stringers and frames need not be as thick as one with larger spaces, and it can weigh less.

In small powerboats, in the 18- to 25-foot range, stringers and frames are frequently a combination of wood and fiber glass. The builder fabricates the frame and stringer system of wood, places it into the hull, and then puts one or more layers of FRP over it. In this system, the wood serves as a male mold for what essentially becomes an FRP frame and stringer system. One builder, for example, builds the latticework for his fishing boats of 1- by 12-inch spruce and then covers it with a layer of chop, a layer of 24-ounce woven roving, and a final layer of chop. The FRP laminate extends several inches from each side of the stringer or frame onto the hull to ensure a good bond. That overlap, of course, also has the effect of increasing the hull thickness in those areas as well. The hull for a 20-foot fisherman designed for speeds of up to 40 mph or so has four longitudinal stringers with transverse frames spaced so that the largest unsupported area is about 4 feet long but only 18 inches wide. The stringers double as timbers for the engine mounts.

This same builder produces high-speed runabouts capable of speeds above 60 mph. The lay-up schedule is essentially the same as that used for the fisherman: a skin coat of 5 ounces of chop followed by three laminates of 24-ounce woven roving and 1.5 ounces of chop in the hull bottom. However, there are significant differences in the stringer and frame systems for the two boats. First, the runabouts use 1-inch-thick plywood rather than the 1-inch spruce for the longitudinal stringers because, the builder says, "the plywood is stronger." Second, the runabouts have more glass reinforcement over the stringers: two laminates of 24-ounce woven roving and 1.5-ounce mat. Third, the laminates for each stringer extend out across the hull bottom so that they overlap the laminates from any adjoining stringers, effectively increasing the hull thickness from the original three laminates to five layers of woven roving and mat.

As boats get larger, stringers and frames become correspondingly larger because the shock loads the hull bottoms must endure increase enormously, particularly with the high-speed motor yachts and sport fishermen (Photos 14 and 15). Even larger sailboats, which may displace 20 or 30 tons, must withstand heavy shock loads when bashing to windward through stormy seas or coming off a large wave on a spinnaker run. Unlike powerboats, however, a sailboat often takes its worst beatings from waves against its side as it sails heeled over, crashing through waves. As a result, large sailboats may need stringers along the sides of the hull, particularly in the forward sections, as well as along the hull bottom.

Another change in stringers and frames also usually occurs as boats get larger: Their construction changes. For example,

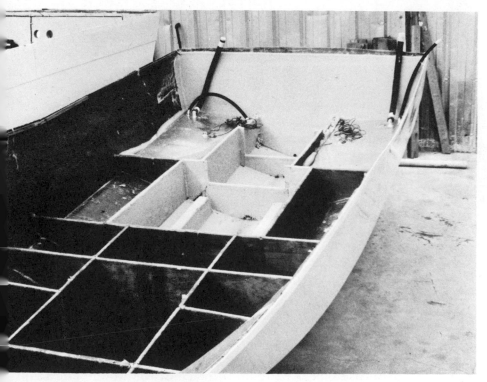

14. A network of plywood stringers and transverse frames serves to stiffen the hull laminate in smaller boats. (Photo by Susan Roberts)

15. Larger boats, as this 43-foot motor yacht, require heavy stringers, frames, and heavy knees at the chines to stiffen hull sections. Usually, these reinforcing members consist of foam-filled FRP laminates. From an engineering perspective, hull thickness is determined by the size of the panels between the frames and stringers. Note the rods fastened across the top of the hull to keep the side panels from spreading. The fillet bond used to fasten the after bulkhead in place is barely visible in the bottom left. (Photo by Susan Roberts)

some builders of larger boats will not use a wood / FRP stringer system, because any gap in the FRP laminates over a wood stringer may allow bilge water into the wood, make it swell, and possibly compromise the structural integrity of the stringer. The larger the boat, of course, the more serious such a problem would be. There are two alternatives to the wood / FRP system. One is to use blocks of foam in place of the wood. The foam serves as a mold for an FRP stringer system to be laid up right in the boat. The foam blocks, of course, are sealed within the stringer system. When a number of hulls of the same design will be built, a more economical system makes use of a reusable male or female mold for the grid system. The grid is laid up using the mold, removed from the mold, and then bonded to the hull. Because stringers and frames laid up in a reusable mold are hollow, they usually are filled with foam after being bonded to the hull. The foam deadens noise and vibrations. It also prevents accumulation and sloshing of water in the stringers.

Foam-cored FRP stringer systems are used particularly in large boats, where the weight and expense of the heavy lumber needed for the very large stringers in such boats make use of wood both impractical and costly. Some builders also are using unidirectional roving or even exotic fiber reinforcement to strengthen stringers systems. One builder, for example, uses three laminates along the stringers in his 60-foot sailboats: the first a layer of triaxial fiber glass roving, the second a layer of unidirectional S-glass roving, and the third a layer of unidirectional carbon fiber roving. The unidirectional roving transmits loads over a longer distance than a woven fabric because nearly all of its fibers are oriented in the same direction. The S-glass and carbon fiber rovings greatly increase the stiffness of the stringer, further helping distribute loads. This sailboat has three stringers on each side. The upper stringers run from the bow about half the length of the hull; the two lower stringers extend the full length of the hull.

HULL LINERS

Hull liners were developed as part of the effort to streamline production lines. An extreme use of a hull liner is most easily illustrated with the Boston Whaler boats. As noted earlier, each Whaler hull consists of an outer shell and an inner shell—or hull liner—designed to fit together to form a single unit. In the Whaler example, the space between the shells is filled with foam both for structural purposes and to provide positive floatation.

Hull liners are used extensively in building both powerboats and sailboats—up to a point. In powerboats, that point generally is in the range of 22 to 24 feet in length. In sailboat construction, the use of full hull liners extends up to about the 40-foot range. In larger boats, hull liners themselves become cumbersome and difficult to handle. As a result, builders are more likely to break the system into smaller components, for example, a fiber glass pan for the cabin sole and, perhaps, settee bases, a separate liner for the head compartment, another for the galley area, and still one more for the forward cabin.

There are generally distinctly different functions served by hull liners used in day sailers, powerboats, and larger sailboats.

• In a day sailer, the hull liner is somewhat analogous to the inner shell of the Boston Whaler; in addition to forming the inner shell of the cockpit and stowage areas, it encloses areas below the deck to provide space for foam floatation.

• In small powerboats, the hull liner most often forms the cockpit sole, steering console, and either the deck or any below-deck accomodations. The liner is usually bonded to the reinforcing framework with a polyester putty and extends up along the inside of the hull to the shear, where it may also be bonded to the hull. The liner may be tied into the hull-to-deck joint as well, usually with self-tapping screws, rivets, or—rarely—bolts. It should be obvious that such a system, properly done, creates a strongly reinforced, unitized structure.

• In sailboats up to about 40 feet in length, the hull liner has been developed to serve as the principal component of all interior accommodations (Photo 16). As a result, it is not unusual to find the cabin sole, galley, settees, cabinets, bookshelves, head, and vee berth all molded into one FRP liner that fits neatly into the hull. However, full hull liners have not proved quite the panacea some had hoped. The reasons include the following: (1) The hull liner must be carefully engineered to fit the hull properly if it is to provide needed structural reinforcement; (2) the molds for such complex shapes are expensive and need long production runs to justify the expense; (3) the builder loses flexibility in changing the interior accommodations; and (4) the taste of the U.S. boating public runs against the shiny plastic look inherent in the use of full hull liners. The last factor has seriously limited the popular appeal of the liner, further

16. A partial hull liner is lifted from its mold. This liner will serve to reinforce the hull of the finished boat and provide the base for much of the interior furnishings. (Photo by Susan Roberts)

detracting from the system's economy by requiring compensatory use of trim, veneers, and decorative fabrics to disguise the FRP surfaces.

Nearly all of these liners are fabricated using a female mold and chopper gun. Seldom does a hull liner have more than a single layer of woven roving. Most often, in fact, the liner is simply laid up using a chopper gun with no woven reinforcing at all. This is because the liner does not need the impact and tensile strength offered by the woven fabric.

Where bulkheads are needed to enclose a forward cabin or head, to provide structural support across the hull against the compressive force of a sailboat's shrouds, or to support a broad expanse of deck, builders often design grooves or flanges into the liner so that a precut plywood bulkhead will fit neatly in place. The bulkhead often is held in place with screws initially. Grooves molded into the deck or headliner help hold the bulkhead firmly in place when the boat is completed (Photos 17 and 18).

Hull liners usually are designed to fit against the hull in specific places to help stiffen hull sections. In fact, one advantage of a well-done hull liner—particularly in sailboat construction—is the opportunity to use a lighter hull lay-up schedule because of the stiffening effect of the liner. Builders generally coat the mating surface of the liner with a polyester resin putty before putting it into the hull. Once the liner is in place, the putty is intended to bond the liner securely to the hull wherever the two surfaces mate.

17. Mold for the headliner of a 35-foot sailboat. Note the groove running across the mold. (Photo by Susan Roberts)

18. In laying up the headliner, the groove in 17 is translated into a flange for positioning and securing the top of the principal interior bulkheads. (Photo by Susan Roberts)

PANS AND HEADLINERS

Use of an FRP pan represents a step back from a full hull liner. Pans are commonly used in larger boats, particularly in sailboat construction. The pan serves essentially as the cabin sole and has molded right into it all of the bumps, dimples, and grooves needed to locate planned interior furnishings. It is bonded to any reinforcing framework in the hull bottom and to the hull around its edge. Some builders, looking for at least some of the advantages hoped for in a full hull liner, may also mold some parts of various interior furniture components into the pan, for example, the base of a settee or the frame for a forward vee berth. Among smaller sailboats, under 30 feet, the pan may even serve as the base for a jig on which the entire interior can be assembled outside the boat while the hull is being laid up. The use of such jigs, however, is generally limited to smaller boats (Photo 19). The size and weight of the assembly increases rapidly with boat size and quickly becomes unmanageable.

19. Increasingly, builders are preassembling interior components outside of the hull to gain assembly line efficiency. At one yard, the interior for one of its smaller boats is assembled on a fiber glass floor pan without the benefit of a jig before being placed into the boat. Note that the veneer has been removed from the bulkheads where they will be bonded to the hull. (Photo by Susan Roberts)

Headliners are needed in FRP boats because the underside of the deck and cabin house are essentially unfinished fiber glass surfaces. For reasons of cost, aesthetics, and weight, headliners today are often made of soft plastic or woven fabrics, usually installed in removable panels. These not only provide a finished look to the overhead, but they also help deaden sound. However, FRP headliners have been common in the past and are still used today in some production boats. In general, headliners are simply sprayed up using a chopper gun.

For practical purposes, an FRP headliner is analogous to a

hull liner: It is used to help stiffen the cabin house and deck assembly and to provide an easily maintained finished interior surface for the overhead, cabin trunk sides, and underside of the deck. Despite the expense of the resin and chopped glass fiber reinforcing materials, the use of an FRP headliner is economical for some builders, particularly where (1) a long production run spreads the cost of the mold across a large number of boats, (2) the builder has used only solid FRP laminates in his hull and deck and does not want to start using cored construction technology for his decks (see Chapter 7), or (3) the builder has maintained a very simple production line to produce a "bare bones" sort of boat. From the point of view of the boat owner, however, the use of an FRP headliner may pose problems of maintenance and repair because of difficulty in gaining access to wiring or fasteners covered by the headliner. It may also sweat in cold weather. On the other side of the ledger, FRP headliners are easy to keep clean.

BONDING COMPONENTS TO THE HULL

Some FRP boats larger than 25 feet are built without the benefit of hull liners and FRP headliners. As a result, all of the interior furnishings and room dividers (bulkheads) should be tied into each other, into the hull, and, where possible, into the deck. There are two reasons for this requirement: First, as noted before, the interior components help provide structural integrity to the overall boat; second, the interior components must be installed so that they will stay put. This means the boat must be able to withstand the rigors of a run across a choppy Gulf Stream or into the short, steep wave system of a stormy Chesapeake Bay without popping a bulkhead or having some piece of cabinetry come loose if a crew member lurches against it. For this reason, a rule of thumb is that all components that touch the hull should be bonded to it. The manner in which these components are bonded to the hull can tell much about the care a builder uses in constructing his boats. This is a part of the boat-building process in which too many builders economize.

Frequently—in fact, inevitably in most boats larger than 25

feet—the interior components of a boat are installed a week or even several weeks after the hull lay-up was completed. Earlier it was mentioned that if more than 48 to 72 hours pass between applying laminates when laying up a hull, the hull surface should be scuff sanded to ensure good adhesion of the new layer of reinforcing fabric. The reason why such sanding is necessary is that after 2 or 3 days, the polyester resin has cured to such a hardness that the new resin has difficulty effecting an acceptable bond. Scuff sanding relieves that problem by giving the new resin a surface to which it can adhere securely. The problem arises when installing interior components. After the hull lay-up is completed, it is usually necessary to scuff sand the hull surface wherever interior components will be bonded to the hull. Such sanding may not be necessary when stringers and frames are installed if the work is done within 48 to 72 hours after the hull lay-up has been completed. Other components, however, usually are installed anywhere from a few days to several weeks later. The adhesion problem is particularly acute if DCPD laminating resins have been used in the hull because of their rapid and very hard cure. For that reason, some builders who use DCPD resins in their lay-up change to a standard laminating resin for the last layer in the laminate.

Bulkheads

Ideally, bulkheads extend right on down to the hull bottom and are attached to the hull from both sides of the bulkhead using a "fillet bond" to avoid creating a "hard spot" in the hull. Such hard spots are undesirable because the hull may flex across the line where the bulkhead meets the hull (Fig. 16), eventually cracking and, finally, failing. The fillet bond, which provides a gentle transition from the hard, relatively sharp edge of a plywood bulkhead to the long flat surface of the hull, usually is made by placing a trapezoidal hat section of foam between the bulkhead and the hull. The trapezoid—a triangle with the top sliced off—forms a gradual turn from the bulkhead to the hull surface (Fig. 17). The bond is then made by laminating one or more layers of reinforcing fabric from the bulkhead onto the

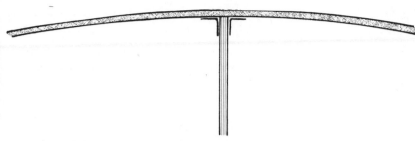

FIG. 16.   If a bulkhead or part of an interior furnishing butts directly against the hull with no effort to spread the load, a hard spot is created. The laminate may fail if the hull panel flexes continually over that spot.

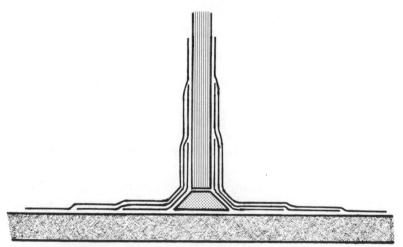

FIG. 17.   A fillet bond between a bulkhead or other vertical edge of interior structure and the hull is best made by placing a trapezoidal section of foam between the edge of the bulkhead and the hull. The foam serves two principal functions. (1) It holds the hard bulkhead away from the hull and (2) it provides a gentle radius for the FRP laminates as they pass from the bulkhead to the hull, spreading the loading over a broader area. In this way, no sharp line is created over which the hull panel will flex.

hull *from both sides of the bulkhead.* This bonding is often called "taping."

A number of builders use only a single layer of woven roving for taping. A better practice calls for using either alternating layers of mat and woven roving or Fabmat. Using mat either separately or as part of the Fabmat as the first layer of the bonding tape against the last hull laminate provides a stronger bond to the hull than will woven roving. Moreover, FRP materials do not adhere well to plywood; the mat surface against the plywood will provide a more uniform bond to the bulkhead. In addition, particularly in boats larger than 25 feet or so, the bond should extend a full 6 inches onto the wood bulkhead and 4 to 6 inches onto the hull. The 6-inch overlap onto the plywood bulkhead is particularly important to compensate for the relatively weak bond between the polyester resin and the plywood. The bond also will be strengthened if the layers of the bonding laminates are "staged," with the first layer of mat and roving extending 2 or 3 inches onto the bulkhead and hull, the second layer extending about 4 inches onto the bulkhead and 3 to 4 inches onto the hull, and a third layer extending a full 6 inches onto the bulkhead and 4 to 6 inches onto the hull. In all cases, as noted earlier, the bulkhead should be taped to the hull from both sides. After the deck has been installed, the bulkheads also should be taped to the overhead. In addition, if the plywood has a veneered surface, the veneer should be cut away where the bond will be made (Photo 20).

Some builders, including some of the better ones, do not use true fillet bonds for bulkhead attachment. Instead, the bulkhead is cut to size, placed in position, and the joint between the hull and bulkhead filled with a caulk or puttylike compound. The joint is then taped as it would be for a fillet bond. In making such joints, however, it is important to use an adequate amount of the "putty" to provide a gentle radius for the turn of the bond from the bulkhead to the hull. Under no circumstances should a gap be left between the edge of the bulkhead and the hull to be bridged by the FRP bonding laminate. Such bonds are particularly vulnerable to failure from impact on the hull because the FRP "bridge" ends up absorbing any impacts, not the bulkhead.

In addition, when composite construction is used in the hull, bulkheads should be bonded to the inner skin of the sandwich. Under no circumstances should the core be removed in the hull lay-up where bulkheads will be placed. The core, you will recall,

20. When a hull is removed from the mold, frequently beams are clamped from one side to the other at locations of structural bulkheads to help maintain the desired hull shape and to position bulkheads for installation. Note how the bulkhead in this photo fits into the partial FRP hull liner and the teak veneer has been removed where the bulkhead will be bonded to the hull. The woven roving bonding the settee base to the hull also is readily visible. (Photo by Susan Roberts)

increases the stiffness of the hull panel. Removing the core along
a line down the side of the hull will weaken the hull along that
line, making the hull panel more flexible right where the edge
of the bulkhead will be placed, and increasing the potential for
eventual hull failure from repeated flexing across the edge of
the bulkhead despite the use of a fillet bond.

Cabin Sole

Whether the cabin sole is formed by an FRP pan or sheet
plywood laid across reinforcing frames or separate floor members, the sole should be bonded securely to the hull around its
entire perimeter. The edges of the sole should be carried right
up to the hull and any gaps filled with foam or putty. The bond
should be made with at least one laminate of 1.5-ounce mat and
24-ounce woven roving, preferably two such laminates in boats
above 30 feet. It generally is not possible to tape the underside
of the sole. By bonding the sole to the hull in this manner, the
cabin sole (or the cockpit deck in an open boat) can be used to
reinforce the hull around much of its length.

Furnishings

Wherever possible, interior furnishings should be bonded to
the hull. They should also be fixed firmly to the cabin sole using
both glue and either boat nails or screws. Bonding furnishings
to the hull serves two functions: It helps stiffen the hull sections, furthering the "unitized" character of the boat construction, and, equally important, it helps ensure that each piece of
furniture will stay put even in the roughest seas. In general,
wherever a vertical piece of a cabinet or settee, or a vertical
divider in a locker, runs up to the hull surface, it should be
bonded to the hull using a fillet bond. Ideally, wherever a horizontal piece of furniture, including fixed shelves in lockers,
runs up to the hull, it too would be bonded to the hull at least
on the upper surface. The exception would be small shelves
located high up under the deck. At that point on the hull—near

the hull–deck joint—the shelves could not reinforce the hull significantly. Nor would the shelves be subject to the kinds of impacts likely to dislodge them.

REINFORCEMENT FOR SAILBOAT MASTS AND RIGGING

Sailboats pose a special challenge to builders: providing the structural support needed to carry the loads from the sails. In most sailboats, these loads are transmitted to the hull through both the mast and the standing rigging, the latter a system of multistranded wires or single-strand extruded rods supporting the mast from bow, stern, and both sides. A relatively small number of boats above 20 feet in length have free-standing masts that have no standing rigging. Such systems rely upon the integral strength of the mast itself to prevent excessive bending or breaking. Support against falling over is provided by the structure of the deck, where the mast passes through it, and by the mast step, which keeps the bottom of the mast from moving in any direction.

Traditionally, masts have been stepped on the boat's keel so that the downward forces created by tightening the standing rigging and from pounding through waves are carried by the heart of the hull's structural framework. Sometimes, however, the mast has been stepped instead on deck; in such systems, mast loads usually are carried by a compression post between the keel and the underside of the deck or cabin top beneath the mast step.

Today, the trend toward high-aspect fin keels has resulted in some boats whose mast steps are at the leading edge of the keel, with the result that loads may be borne by the hull laminate in a relatively small area rather than by the entire keel section. This development has presented a challenge to builders to reinforce the mast step adequately. Some such boats, including some from highly regarded builders, have developed leaks around the area of the mast step from the repeated pounding of the mast against its step, absorbed by the laminate when racing to windward in choppy seas with a highly tensioned rig.

Loads exerted by standing rigging are of two sorts: direct vertical pull and compression or "squeezing" loads between opposing parts of the rigging. An illustration of squeezing loads is seen in lightweight racers equipped with backstay tensioners. It is not uncommon for backstays to be overtightened so that they actually bend the hull of such boats along its fore-and-aft axis, banana-like. Efforts to stiffen hulls against such forces have included encapsulating steel pipe along the center line of the hull as a fore-and-aft stiffener. More conventional approaches to preventing such distortion include production of stiffer hull sections and use of structural frame and stringer systems to reinforce the hull.

Similar compressive forces are created between the two sides of the hull in the area of the mast by the intermediate and upper shrouds. There has been a gradual change in the manner in which builders handle shroud loads. In traditional boats, shrouds are attached to strong metal straps bolted to the exterior of the hull. In the mid to late 1970s, the effort by designers to develop boats that sail closer to the wind resulted in moving chain plates inboard—often as much as a foot or more in from the rail, depending upon boat size and design. One result is that jibs can be sheeted in tighter, improving windward performance. Another result, however, has been a need to change the manner in which chain plates were attached.

In both inboard and outboard chain plate systems, the compressive loadings of the upper shrouds are carried by a strong bulkhead usually located right at the mast's position. At a minimum, the bulkhead is made using ¾-inch plywood in a boat between about 30 and 40 feet in length, thicker in a larger boat, down to ½-inch plywood between about 20 and 30 feet.

With outboard chain plates bolted to the hull, the principal function of this main bulkhead is to resist the squeezing load of the shrouds. With inboard chain plate systems, the chain plates for upper and intermediate shrouds are bolted to the bulkhead. As a result, the bulkhead not only carries the squeezing loads, but also the vertical loads of the shrouds.

The advent of inboard chain plate systems has also meant a change in the attachment of lower shrouds, usually to chain plates bolted to knees (partial bulkheads) bonded to the hull and deck. Insofar as the upward forces on chain plates conceivably can gradually begin to work chain plate bolts in their holes, builders should use FRP pads to reinforce the plywood used to make the main bulkhead and knees. The hard FRP pads will keep the bolt holes in the relatively soft plywood from becoming enlarged after a time.

More recently, as part of the effort to improve sailing performance by reducing boat weight, some builders have done away with knees and bulkheads as anchors for shrouds. In their place, these builders are using tie rods to connect chain plate deck fittings to a structural frame-and-stringer grid in the hull bottom. The idea behind this arrangement is that anchoring the shrouds to the structural grid will spread rigging loads throughout the hull bottom. Anchoring them in the grid also reduces the "squeezing" forces from the shrouds. The tie rod system also allows designers greater freedom in their use of interior space because they are not forced to work around a midship's main bulkhead.

7

The Deck and Cabin House
Topping Off the Outer Shell

The construction of a boat's deck and cabin house can be as critical to its safety and performance as the construction of its hull. This is an area, however, often ignored by a boating public more interested in the convenience of the deck layout and the view from the cabin than in the structural integrity of this upper shell of their boat. So long as the deck feels solid underfoot, it passes structural inspection; and yet this is the portion of an FRP boat—from the hull-to-deck joint on up—in which one is most likely to have leaks and other minor problems. In survival conditions offshore, it may also be a likely area of structural failure.

On small boats, the deck, cabin house, and cockpit liners often are molded in one piece using only a chopper gun. The cockpit liner portion usually has good support. Wherever it mates with the hull, the liner and hull panel are mutually reinforcing. In addition, the cockpit liner is tied into the boat's system of frames and stringers. The deck and cabin house portion of these moldings, however, usually have much less support. As a result, they are seldom intended to carry much weight, for example, the weight of a 200-pound person stepping down from a dock.

By the time boats reach about 25 feet in length, most builders are using some kind of a core material in the deck and cabin top—wherever people walk. In a relatively few larger boats, the core material is used throughout the sides of the cabin trunk as well. The strength of the cabin house is particularly important in sailboats intended for offshore use where, in extreme conditions, the deck and cabin structure may have to withstand the force of a breaking wave or of the boat being thrown by a wave onto its side.

Of course, another benefit of a cored deck is its insulation value. One problem that has plagued FRP boats in cold climates since the first glass boat was built is the formation of condensation on the inside of the boat. A fully cored deck and cabin trunk provide important insulation and generally eliminate problems of condensation on the overhead.

Perhaps the most widely used core material in deck structures is plywood. The most costly core for decks is Nomex honeycomb. Between the two are end-grain balsa, Airex and Klegecell foams, and Coremat. One large-volume powerboat builder uses a low-cost open-cell PVC foam in "nonstructural areas" of the decks of some of his boats. As noted earlier, the use of open-cell foam as a core material is contrary to generally accepted practice.

Even where balsa or a foam core is used, most builders substitute plywood coring wherever deck fittings from bow rails to handrails, cleats to Genoa tracks, and anchor windlass to sheet winches will be bolted to the deck (Fig. 18). The reasons for substituting the plywood differ. In a deck cored with Airex or Klegecell foam, the plywood is used because of its compressive strength. The bolts can be tightened down snugly without concern about distorting the core material. In a deck cored with balsa, the reason most often given is to isolate the balsa core from a possible leak around the deck fitting. This logic is questionable. If water gets into the plywood, it will do more damage than if it gets into the balsa, if one assumes that both are applied properly. The reason is that the grain of the wood will spread water throughout the piece of plywood, which may be as large as 6 inches square. The grain of the balsa will not spread the water but, instead, will confine it to the source of the leak.

The uncored deck of a small boat may receive some reinforcing from the use of stringers or, if there is a small cabin, a head-

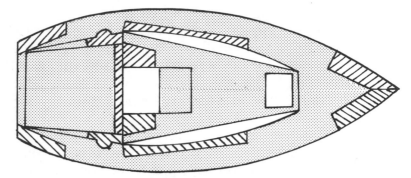

FIG. 18. This deck plan for a 30-foot sloop shows where plywood core is used in place of the foam (or balsa) core used for the remainder of the deck. Note that in this boat the sides of the cabin trunk are not cored. The core also is left out where the two hatches will be installed.

liner. The headliner can be designed to mate with the underside of the deck laminate, thereby reinforcing the deck surface. In larger boats, the headliner's function is often merely cosmetic. The underside of the headliner can have virtually any surface texture molded into the gel coat, giving a finished look to the overhead right out of the mold. As noted in Chapter 6, some builders—but not all—also use the headliner to anchor the tops of bulkheads in place. These headliners are molded with grooves designed to fit over the edge of bulkheads and other interior furnishings, providing important structural support to interior elements as well as to the cabin house and deck.

Although the use of a headliner may be economical for the builder, it may ultimately prove costly to the boat owner. Often builders attach all deck fittings before the headliner is installed. As a result, it may not be possible to get at the underside of a deck fitting without cutting through the headliner should one of those fittings need to be taken up or replaced. Moreover, a headliner may make it impossible for a buyer to determine whether the builder has used self-tapping screws, machine screws (bolts), lock washers, or backing plates with any of the deck fittings. Servicing or replacing wiring installed between the liner and the deck also may be difficult.

Of course, it is possible to build a strong deck using a solid

FRP laminate. For example, the CSY sailboats built during the late 1970s had solid fiber glass decks that are probably as strong as most cored decks on similarly sized boats. However, the thickness of the laminate—about ½ inch for the deck of the CSY 44, for example—put what many designers would consider an excessive amount of weight high in the boat. However, as CSY loudly proclaimed, their decks will never have any of the problems of waterlogged cores or delamination that are possible in cored decks if the lay-up is not applied properly.

A sharp contrast to the solid FRP laminate of the CSY deck is offered by the lay-up schedules for the decks of two smaller sailboats (Fig. 19):

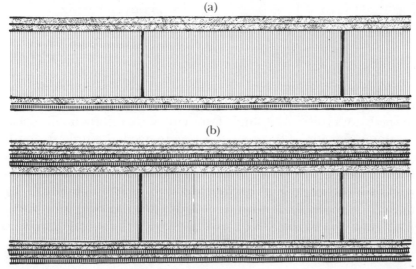

FIG. 19. (a) The lay-up schedule for the deck of a 30-foot racer/cruiser made using a ½-inch end-grain balsa core specifies two layers of 1.5-ounce mat as the outer skin and a 1.5-ounce mat/18-ounce woven roving laminate as the inner skin. The woven roving is placed on the underside of the structure to help carry the tensile loads created, for example, when people walk on the deck. (b) The lay-up schedule for the deck of a 36-foot offshore cruising cutter also made using ½-inch end-grain balsa core calls for an outer skin consisting of two layers of ¾-ounce mat, two ¾-ounce mat/18-ounce woven roving laminates, and a layer of 1.5-ounce mat as bedding for the core, and an inner skin consisting of one layer of ¾-ounce mat against the core and two ¾-ounce/18-ounce woven roving laminates as the inner skin.

30-foot racer / cruiser	*36-foot cruising cutter*
Gel coat	Gel coat
1.5-oz mat	¾-oz mat
1.5-oz mat	¾-oz mat
½-in. balsa core	¾-oz mat
1.5-oz mat	18-oz woven roving
18-oz woven roving	¾-oz mat
	18-oz woven roving
	1.5-oz mat
	½-in. balsa core
	¾-oz mat
	¾-oz mat
	18-oz woven roving
	¾-oz mat
	18-oz woven roving

Two points are of interest: The heavier lay-up schedule for the cruising cutter reflects its intended use for offshore sailing, and in the racer cruiser, the single laminate of woven roving is placed on the underside of the deck to provide needed tensile strength. The rationale is easily understood if one assumes that most loadings on the deck are downward forces, as when someone walks on the deck. For a cored deck to bend under load, the underside of the deck must stretch or tear; the long continuous filament fibers of the woven roving provide the strength needed to minimize such stretching or tearing (Photos 21 and 22).

On large motor yachts, builders are confronted by engineering challenges that extend above what we normally think of as the deck—for example, the hard tops which cover main deck and salon areas, but which also must serve as a deck themselves. It is enough here to illustrate one such challenge and one builder's solution. His 48-foot motor yacht has a hard top that measures 15 feet by 14 feet and is supported by only four corner posts. The hard top must be capable of supporting a minimum of 1,350 pounds. This particular builder has engineered a composite structure that weighs only 550 pounds by using a Klegecell foam core and carbon fiber reinforcement in the underneath FRP skin.

21. Gel coat already has been applied to this deck mold and workers are now applying a skin coat using a chopper gun. Note the strands of roving being fed through the workers' hands to the chopper gun.

22. After applying the chop to a small section, workers use grooved metal rollers to roll out the laminate, compressing it from a wet fluff an inch or more thick to a compact laminate layer of about $5/100$ of an inch in thickness. (Photos by Susan Roberts)

CORE MATERIALS FOR DECKS

The practice of coring decks has been around for many years. There are two very different reasons for this. From a marketing standpoint, the use of the core has offered the most cost-effective method for making a deck strong enough that it feels sturdy underfoot when a prospective buyer walks on the deck or cabin top. From a design standpoint, the core has offered needed strength without the extra weight topsides that results from using a solid FRP laminate thick enough to do the same job.

All of the commonly accepted core materials can be used effectively; however, each has characteristics that may offer specific advantages or pose specific disadvantages in different applications.

Plywood

Over the years, plywood has probably been the most commonly used core material for decks. The procedure is simple enough: Squares and rectangles of plywood ranging from 1 or 2 inches to about 6 inches on a side are placed one by one into the mold between layers of mat or, more likely, chop (Photo 23). Where weight is not at issue, plywood can be used effectively to make a good, solid strong deck. For example, among sailboats it has been common to see plywood used in the decks of heavy displacement cruising yachts, though considerably less so to see it used in racing boats. One potential problem with a plywood core, as mentioned earlier, involves moisture. A number of boats with plywood-cored decks have developed serious problems of core delamination because of moisture in the plywood. This problem has been most common among boats built in the Far East.

From the builders' viewpoint, plywood has been a core of choice principally because of cost and convenience. Since the interiors of most FRP boats traditionally have been fabricated from ½-inch plywood, builders often have had sufficient scrap right at hand to cut into squares and rectangles for coring their

23. Blocks of ½-inch plywood often are used as a core to stiffen walking surfaces of a deck. The blocks of plywood are put down into a wet layer of mat or, in this case, chop. (Photo by Susan Roberts)

decks. As a result, many have been able to avoid purchasing separate materials for the deck core. Today those advantages are disappearing, partly because builders are doing better jobs and partly because of changing technology. One powerboat builder, for example, comments that his shop has become so good at planning use of their ½-inch plywood that they no longer have enough scrap to core their decks. As a result, that builder is changing to ⅜-inch plywood for his deck core to reduce his costs. At other yards, many of the components formerly constructed of plywood are now being molded into hull liners, further reducing the plywood scrap available for coring the deck.

End-Grain Balsa

Today, end-grain balsa may well have surpassed plywood as the most commonly used core material for building decks. There are several reasons: The balsa core is considerably lighter than plywood. The balsa core material also costs less than plywood, Airex, or Klegecell. The balsa cored deck is considerably stronger than a foam-cored deck (unless extra FRP laminates are added to the underside of the foam-cored deck, adding to weight and cost). And, because we are now talking about the deck, there is not the old bugaboo about water that still haunts balsa's use in hulls—at least, not to the same degree. As noted earlier, many builders still remove the balsa core wherever there will be a deck fitting, replacing the balsa core either with a solid FRP laminate or with plywood. In any case, deck fittings must be well bedded to prevent leaks. In addition, wherever a hole is drilled or cut through the deck or cabin house, better builders seal the core carefully, using either laminating resin, gel coat, or a good sealant. Unfortunately, sealing the core in this manner is sometimes neglected, as a glance under the chain pipe of many boats will reveal.

Klegecell Foam

When light weight is the most important criterion and the builder is restricted to today's conventional materials and technology, Klegecell foam is the core of choice in the deck. Klegecell is lighter in weight than both balsa and Airex. While not as strong as balsa, it is considerably stronger—stiffer—than Airex. As a result, Klegecell is used frequently in racing sailboats.

Although Klegecell is not subject to damage should water leak around a deck fitting, it can be crushed. As a result, special attention still is necessary wherever deck fitting are installed. For example, wherever deck fittings will be subject to high stress, the Klegecell foam is removed and replaced either with plywood core or a solid laminate. Such fittings may include cleats for the anchor line or dock lines, handrails, Genoa tracks, pedestal steering base, winches, or an anchor windlass. When lighter stresses are involved, spacer tubes are used to prevent workers from crushing the core when tightening bolts.

Airex Foam

For a long time, Airex was not widely used in decks because of concern that it would deform under the kind of temperatures one could easily exceed if a colored deck—for example, a tan-colored deck—were exposed to the tropical sun. The cause of that concern has been removed; the foam has been reformulated to increase its heat tolerance. As a result, Airex foam is finding wider use today in deck structures.

However, Airex still has an inherent disadvantage compared to either end-grain balsa or Klegecell as a deck core. That disadvantage is its flexibility—the same flexibility that often makes Airex attractive for use in hulls. Although the use of Airex imparts superior impact resistance to the composite, one or more extra laminates are needed in the inner skin of the Airex composite (compared to composites using plywood, balsa, or Klegecell) to provide needed stiffness. These extra laminates add both weight and cost to the deck. The flexibility of Airex foam also makes precautions similar to those required with Klegecell imperative wherever deck fittings are attached. Although the Airex core will not crush, it can be compressed easily.

Coremat

In the endless effort among builders to find ways for reducing costs, Coremat is likely to find increasing application in decks among builders who do not want to go to the expense of using more conventional core materials. Builders of some small boats, for example, now use Coremat in place of a layer of fiber glass fabric to stiffen their otherwise solid FRP deck laminates by increasing its thickness some 4 or 5 millimeters. Even builders of larger boats are using Coremat to help stiffen their decks

One large builder, for example, uses a combination of Coremat and deck shape without benefit of frames, stringers, or wood or foam core to stiffen the 20-foot-long foredeck on one of his 60+ mile per hour boats. The Coremat, which goes down just like a layer of chopped strand mat, adds to the deck panel stiffness by increasing the laminate thickness 4 millimeters (slightly less than ³/₁₆ of an inch) (Photo 24). Additional stiffening is provided by the shape of a slightly raised section running down the

24. The two relatively thick, fuzzy white layers in the laminate shown in this cutout for a hatch assembly are layers of Coremat used to stiffen the deck section. The Coremat helps give the deck a solid feel underfoot; it does not, however, contribute significantly to the strength of the laminate. (Photo by Susan Roberts)

center line for the full length of the deck. The Coremat deck is lighter than either a plywood-cored deck or a solid FRP laminate of equal thickness would be, but heavier than a comparable balsa deck. Although use of a plywood, balsa, Airex, or Klegecell core would make a stronger deck, Coremat offers significant cost savings in labor and materials compared to the other core materials, and the deck strength is said to be sufficient for the use it receives.

Nomex Honeycomb

The use of Nomex honeycomb offers the highest strength-to-weight ratio of any other core material used in construction of decks today. However, the honeycomb material itself is costly and the lay-up technology is beyond the capability of most boat builders. As noted earlier, honeycomb is best suited for use with epoxy prepregs, which must be vacuum bagged and cured in an oven after the lay-up has been completed. At this time, the only "production" boats constructed using Nomex honeycomb in their decks are Stiletto catamarans. The honeycomb has been used, however, in both the deck and other components of high-speed boats built specially for the offshore racing circuit. Additionally, builders of some production powerboats are experimenting with Nomex honeycomb in both their hulls and decks (see Chapter 12).

DECK SURFACES

A sometimes neglected but important part of deck construction is its surface finish. People must be able to walk on the deck in fair weather or foul without slipping. Two methods for providing a nonskid surface are used widely today. One involves molding a nonskid pattern into the gel coat of the deck surface; the other involves applying a nonskid surface made of another material.

One common pattern molded into the gel coat of a fiber glass deck over the years has consisted of small diamonds. This diamond pattern has been only marginally effective. A somewhat more effective nonskid pattern resembles the kind of surface that would be left by rolling a paint roller over a tacky surface or by scattering a light sprinkling of coarse sand onto the gel coat. This second pattern provides a more effective nonskid surface, particularly when the crew is wearing boat shoes. However, neither pattern is particularly effective when the deck is wet and the crew is barefoot. Of course, both patterns will gradually be worn smooth from use.

A highly effective alternative is provided by nonskid mats

made from mixtures of cork and rubber. Available patterns include raised diamonds and round nubs resembling the cups on an octopus's leg. Both patterns provide good traction wet or dry. Nonskid mats of this sort are being used by an increasing number of builders. Because these mats come in any of several colors, they add a spot of color to boat decks as well as improved safety. However, in tropical areas, the lightest available colors are suggested to prevent the nonskid mats from acting as a solar heat collector.

HULL-TO-DECK JOINTS

There are few areas of boat construction that have been argued about more than the matter of attaching a boat's deck to its hull. If there is a consensus among builders as to what method of making that hull-to-deck joint is best, it is not evident in their products. Some generalities can be made, however. Most naval architects seem to agree the strongest hull-to-deck joint is one in which the deck is bolted at about 4-inch intervals to an inward-turning hull flange. A less satisfactory joint is fastened with self-tapping screws. The most popular method of making hull-to-deck joints among builders of smaller boats seems to rely on pop rivets to attach the deck to the hull. In addition, some builders rely either on fiber glass materials alone or on some combination of mechanical fastener and fiber glass materials to make their hull-to-deck joints.

In the production process, work on the hull and deck proceeds on roughly parallel schedules. The deck, of course, usually requires less time. The lay-up is lighter and outfitting the deck is generally less complex than building in the interior of the hull. However, before the deck is mated to the hull, everything that can be completed is done: Hatches are installed; deck hardware is mounted; wiring is run; windows are installed in the cabin trunk; the headliner—if any—is installed; and all teak trim is finished out. The object is to complete everything that can be done while the deck is still at ground level where it is easy to work on; once it is on the boat, many underneath areas are difficult to reach.

When mechanical fasteners are used to make the hull-to-deck joint, there are several basic steps. The deck is first placed on the hull without sealant so that the holes needed to accommodate fasteners—rivets, self-tapping screws, or bolts—can be predrilled. This also provides a last opportunity to make certain all interior components fit properly under the deck or into the headliner. Once the fitting work has been completed and all holes drilled, the deck often is removed so that the mating surfaces on both the hull and deck can be trimmed if necessary and cleaned thoroughly to remove any remaining mold release agent, resin surfacing agent, dust, dirt, or grease. The mating surfaces may also be rough-sanded to help ensure that the sealant adheres well to both surfaces.

Once surface preparations have been completed, the sealant is applied liberally. Many builders use either a polyurethane adhesive / sealant or a polysulfide sealant in the hull-to-deck joint; others use less expensive sealants; and some use a layer of chopped strand mat liberally soaked with polyester resin to seal the joint and to help bond the deck to the hull. In any case, once the sealant has been applied, the deck is lowered onto the hull, and the job of tying the two together begins.

Some builders prefer to rely completely or partially upon FRP materials to tie the hull and deck together. However, many in the industry are concerned that it is not possible to check the adequacy of a hull-to-deck joint that relies principally or wholly upon the chemical bond of an FRP laminate for its continuity. The reason for this is that the strength of an FRP hull-to-deck joint depends upon how well each of the the steps involved in surface preparation and the actual joint lamination are carried out. There is, however, no means available after the work has been completed to determine whether it was done properly.

The obvious objective in using a chemically bonded hull-to-deck joint is achieving a unified FRP structure. In principle, such a structure should be strong and watertight. In practice, however, the joint relies upon a bond often made under the worst of circumstances in terms of the accessibility needed to apply the FRP materials and the surface conditions required to achieve a good bond, if one assumes the materials are properly applied. Moreover, the bond's strength relies in part on the area of overlap, how far above and below the actual joint the bonding laminate is carried. Depending upon the size of the boat, the bonding laminate should extend from 2 to 6 or more inches above and below the joint. It is often difficult, however, to achieve more than the minimum overlap because of simple space limitations or the intrusion of cabinetry or even fasteners from deck hardware.

Surface preparation is particularly critical to ensuring a good bond between the new laminate and the final layers of the hull and deck laminates. To aid that bond, some builders lay up the last laminates of their hull and deck with a resin that does not have a surfacing agent (wax). Without that wax, the resin in the last laminate remains slightly tacky, presenting a better surface for coming back later to bond items to the hull and deck—or, in this case, the hull to the deck. The disadvantage, however, is that the tacky surfaces collect whatever dust is in the area. The surface must be cleaned thoroughly with a solvent before laminating. In this instance, sanding to clean or roughen the surface is impractical because the tacky resin tends to gum up the grinding disk. On the other hand, if a surfacing agent is used in the laminating resin and, therefore, the hull and deck laminates have cured completely, thorough sanding with a coarse grinding disk is standard procedure to clean and roughen the surfaces so that the new resin will bond well when the fiber glass tape is applied.

The strongest hull-to-deck joints are made on a horizontal plane. The reason for this is that the heaviest loadings on the hull-to-deck joint are generally vertical, for example, the shock loads from the hull pounding through waves. When the deck rests on a horizontal surface molded into the hull, neither the fasteners in a mechanical joint nor the resin bond in a chemical joint has to carry the brunt of these shock loads. Instead, those loads are transmitted directly from the hull to the deck. If the overlap of the hull and deck is on a vertical plane, however, the full force of any such loads falls upon the material used to fasten the two moldings together. These forces have a tendency to make fasteners work in their holes through the laminate in a mechanical joint. They also apply heavy shear stresses across the resin bond of a chemical joint (Fig. 20). Both horizontal and vertical joints are used in the industry.

Horizontal Plane Hull-to-Deck Joints

There are two possible horizontal flanges that can be molded into the hull. The easier and, therefore, the less costly, is a flange that turns outward. The more difficult and more costly alternative is a flange that turns inward (Fig. 20). As noted in Chapter 3, it costs more to mold the inner flange in part because the mold itself is more complex.

The outer hull flange is popular among some builders for two principal reasons. It provides an easy joint for using pop rivets. Moreover, once the rivets have been installed, the joint

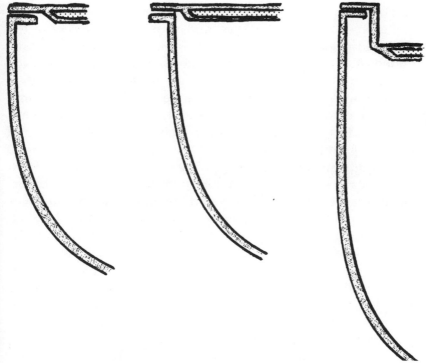

FIG. 20.   Horizontal plane hull-to-deck joints.

can be covered with a rubber molding that serves the dual function of protecting the joint and providing a rub rail. For builders who use fiber glass to either make or help make the hull-to-deck joint, the outward-turning flange also provides a smooth inner surface along the joint to apply a fiber glass tape. The only screw or bolt ends coming down through the deck to get in the way of the fiber glass material are from deck fittings. However, the outer flange has one major disadvantage: It is vulnerable to impact damage from bumping up against pilings.

Perhaps because of the vulnerability factor, most larger boats use an inner flange to effect the hull-to-deck joint. In most instances, the joints rely principally upon self-tapping screws, bolts, or both screws and bolts to maintain their integrity. In some instances, builders may also apply fiber glass reinforcing to help strengthen the joint. The use of the fiber glass in this instance, however, poses some disadvantages. The fiber glass material is difficult to apply in the first place because the various cabinets, shelves, lockers, and so on, block access to the inside of the joint. The hull and deck laminates should be scuff-sanded or, if done earlier, wiped down thoroughly to provide a clean surface for the bond, but the interior structure makes such surface preparation difficult at best and likely to be omitted. Added to that, the frequency of the screw or bolt ends coming down through the flange (about every 4 inches, and more frequently if both bolts and self-tappers have been used) compounds the difficulty of applying the reinforcement neatly, because each screw or bolt end becomes a miniature tent pole. The result frequently is sloppy and one must question just how much strength such fiber glass reinforcement adds to the joint. In addition, the fiber glass material will make any future efforts to locate and repair a leak in the hull-to-deck joint extremely difficult. Despite all of those negative factors, however, some builders believe the potentially strongest hull-deck joint is made by bedding the joint well with an adhesive / sealent, fastening the joint with self-tapping screws, applying a fiber glass bond across the laminate, and then bolting the joint.

In boats with an FRP bulwark integral to the hull and deck, the joint is generally made at the top of the bulwark. Most builders apply the sealant, use self-tapping screws to make the joint fast, and then cap the bulwark with teak. In some boat-yards, the cap rail is attached with self-tapping screws; in others, machine screws (bolts) are used to attach the cap rail, thereby effecting a bolted hull-to-deck joint.

Among sailboats, bulwarks are less common. The flat outer edge of the deck simply mates to the inner flange. It is usually held in position with self-tapping screws until the sealant is at least partially cured, after which a slotted aluminum or teak toe rail is installed along the joint. The bolts used to fasten down the toe rail also effect a bolted hull-to-deck joint.

There is still a third manner in which inner flanges are used to make hull-to-deck joints. There is no bulwark or separate toe rail involved. Instead, a low toe rail is molded into the laminate an inch or so from the outer edge of the deck. The builder may use either self-tapping screws or bolts to effect the joint; in either case, the fasteners are placed outboard of the molded toe rail. The heads of the fasteners usually are covered by trim or a rubber molding.

Vertical Plane Hull-to-Deck Joints

The most common form of a vertical plane hull-to-deck joint is the so-called "shoe box" joint (Fig. 21). In this construction, the deck is molded with a downward flange along the outer edge. In effect, the deck looks like the top of a shoe box. It is placed over the hull, which has no flange, like the top fits over the bottom part of a shoe box. A sealant, sometimes simply a polyester putty, is forced up under the edge of the descending deck flange, which is then usually fastened to the hull with metal fasteners, most often pop rivets, sometimes self-tappers, and seldom bolts. The rivets or screws may also be used to attach an extruded trim piece along the flange. The trim covers up the joint and is fitted with a rubber molding to act as a rub rail.

A variation of the shoe box-style joint uses both a descending deck flange and an inward-turning hull flange. In this instance, the descending flange of the deck serves only one purpose: to

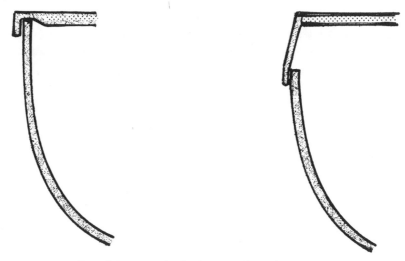

FIG. 21.   Vertical plane hull-to-deck joints.

ensure the proper shape of the hull at the shear. After the deck has been joined to the inner hull flange, the descending deck flange is removed.

Another variation of the shoe box hull-to-deck joint has been used principally on sailboats in which the designer increases the interior volume of the boat by adding several inches to the descending deck flange. This device is used for two reasons: It lets a builder use an existing hull to produce a new model having increased interior space, thereby saving the expense of building a new hull mold; the added space is obtained simply by using a long descending flange to raise the deck. The second reason involves aesthetics. A designer can create the illusion of a lower (less boxy) hull line by creating an artificial shear line along a joint several inches or more below deck level.

Some boats designed in this style may have small (horizontal plane) outer flanges along both the hull and deck. If so, of course, those flanges may add significantly to the strength of the joint. If there are no horizontal flanges, this kind of hull-to-deck joint places major stresses on any rivets, self-tapping screws, or bolts used to bond the joint. However, this style joint can be designed to provide optimum opportunity to effect an FRP bond because the distance above as well as below the joint provides the large surface area needed for such a bond. Once the bonding laminates have been applied, mechanical fasteners may also be used to help guard against potential shear forces causing failure of the resin bond.

8

Marine Sealants
Stopping Tomorrow's Leaks Today

Had wood boat builders had access 30 years ago to some of the sealants available to the modern boating industry today, some of the impetus for bringing fiber glass technology to the boating world might have been lost. Just as one example, the wooden boat enthusiast today can caulk his hull, follow up by filling the seams with a modern polysulfide sealant, and then quit worrying about his seams for several years. A slight exaggeration? Perhaps, but only slight. Today's polysulfide sealants adhere strongly to the wood planks, expand and contract up to 25 percent as the wood alternately swells and shrinks when the boat is put into and taken out of the water, and remain flexible year after year. Another example is that no longer must the wood boat owner be plagued by old-fashioned bedding compounds that dry out or harden after a season or two and then let rain water seep through window frames, under toe rails, and under deck fittings into inaccessible areas, creating conditions ripe for dry rot. He can now choose from several different modern sealants for use as bedding compounds, all of which promise to remain flexible and retain their watertight seal year after year.

The emergence of fiber glass boats, of course, quickly eliminated problems of leaking hull seams for those who chose the new technology. But as all too many owners of older and even some new FRP boats know, the problems of deck and cabin house leaks have been much more difficult to overcome. However, the variety of sealants and adhesive / sealants available to the marine industry today offers promise of truly "dry" boats— boats in which water comes in only through open hatches, ports, and other ventilating devices not closed off to spray or foul weather in a timely manner. And that promise is not for the future; it is for today. Builders need only be willing to spend the money for the sealant best suited for each use, and to spend the time ensuring that the sealant is properly used on the production line.

There are seven basic varieties of sealants and adhesive / sealants sold to the marine industry today (Table 5). At one end of the spectrum are the traditional oil-based caulks or bedding compounds that some in the industry believe are no longer suited for marine use (except for their price). At the other end is a secret formula that its manufacturer claims is far and away the best adhesive / sealant on the market today—better even than the polysulfides mentioned earlier.

Whether the promise of modern sealants is realized in any particular boat, of course, is up to the builder. One factor he considers carefully is cost, and rightly so. Some obviously choose to conserve costs with their choice of sealants. For example, in 1982 we looked at a 37-foot sailboat as it was being commissioned and found the builder had sealed the hull-to-deck joint with an oil-based material that had the consistency of window putty. That boat, which had a price tag of about $90,000, is almost certainly destined to have a leaky hull-to-deck joint. Even more recently, at the end of a boat show, we sat on a 36-foot production sailboat, which was selling then for about $110,000, and listened to the frustrated dealer describe a variety of leaks that had water running over the cabin sole every time there was a hard rain—leaks he was completely unable to trace back to their sources. By way of contrast, other builders go to an opposite extreme. One we visited has only one adhesive / sealant in his plant and it was one of the more expensive sealants on the market. Although he admits the product is overkill for many uses, by having only one sealant in the plant he eliminates the possibility of having the wrong sealant used in a critical appli-

Table 5   Properties of Different Types of Sealants

Oil Base	Butyl rubber	Acrylic latex	Silicone
Easy cleanup	Fast cure	Easy cleanup	Good adhesion
Low cost	Good weather resistance	Good weather resistance	Poor water resistance
Suitable only as bedding compound	Paintable	Paintable	Not paintable
Consistency of putty	Suitable only as bedding compound	Suitable as bedding compound or filler	Not suitable for use on boat exterior above or below waterline
Needs replacing after relatively few years	Not suited for use underwater	Poor water resistance	Not suitable for use where cut off from air (will not cure)
	Not suited for joints that will move	Good resistance to oil; poor resistance to fuels	
	Vulnerable to fuels and lubricating oils		

cation. Most builders, of course, fall between the two extremes. In addition to cost, of course, builders often consider other factors as well in choosing sealants. These include ease of application, how fast the sealant sets up, ease of clean up, and whether the sealant can be painted.

OIL-BASE CAULKS AND BEDDING COMPOUNDS

The most common example of these materials, and one that almost everyone can recognize, is window putty. These caulks consist of a mixture of fish oils, vegetable oil, talc (calcium carbonate), and a solvent to give desired viscosity. The products

Silicone/acrylic	Polysulfides	Polyurethanes
Good adhesion	Excellent adhesive properties	Excellent adhesive properties
Fair water resistance	Excellent water resistance	Excellent water resistance
Suitable as bedding for deck fittings, windows, hatches	Suitable for use above *and* below waterline	Suitable for use above *and* below waterline
Not suited for use below waterline	Does not shrink in curing	Very tough
Tough; can be sanded when cured	Remains elastic	Remains elastic
Paintable	Paintable	Exceptional service life
	Good resistance to fuels and oils	Vulnerable to some teak cleaners; not recommended as sealant in teak decks
	Exceptional service life	
	Good weather resistance	
	Not suited for use with aluminum	

have been around for well over 50 years and the basic formula has changed little in that time. Some in the industry today argue that these so-called "oleo-base resins" have been left behind by technology and should no longer be used in the marine industry. Their rationale is that the only advantage offered by oil-based caulks is cost; for a little more money, much better products are available.

The manufacturers of these caulks, however, maintain that their products offer boat owners and builders good, low-cost bedding compounds for sealing cleats and other deck fittings against leaks. They are not intended, however, for seams or joints subject to movement.

Oil-based caulks and bedding compounds are very slow-drying products and can be used above or below the waterline. However, they will cure completely over a period of a few years, becoming hard and crumbly. For this reason, they probably should not be used where the dried out caulk cannot be replaced easily, for example, in hull-to-deck joints or in bedding ports and hatches.

BUTYL RUBBER SEALANTS

Butyl rubber sealants are recommended principally for bedding hardware and deck fittings. They adhere moderately well to fiber glass, aluminum, steel, and wood. However, butyl rubber sealants should not be used in joints that will have much movement; although these sealants will stretch, they have poor recovery properties. These compounds also should not be used where they will be exposed to gasoline, diesel fuel, kerosene, or motor oil, as they have poor resistance to fuel and oil. They also are not suited for use in underwater seams or joints.

Butyl rubber sealants offer the advantages of a fast cure, good weather resistance, and of being easily painted. Moreover, they do not shrink when curing. Some butyl rubber sealants have been formulated so that they can be applied easily without "hairs" forming when the tube is pulled away from the bead. Those that make such "hairs" or "strings" create cleanup problems. Most butyl rubber sealants require a solvent containing either toluene or xylene for cleanup. If an excess of the sealant exists, it can be trimmed off easily with a knife.

ACRYLIC LATEX SEALANTS

Acrylic latex sealants are recommended for use principally as a filler or as a bedding compound for deck fittings and hardware. As a filler, however, acrylic latex sealants should not be used in areas having much joint movement. Use of acrylic latex sealants as a bedding compound should be restricted to applications having only a relatively light exposure to water, because they have relatively poor resistance to water. They certainly should never be used below the waterline. They are probably best not used in a windshield that is exposed to frequent heavy spray. Nor would they be recommended for bedding a through-hull fitting above the waterline that might be exposed to frequent wetting from the wave action of the water. Although acrylic latex sealants have generally good resistance to oil, they have poor resistance to fuels.

If one recognizes those limitations, acrylic latex sealants offer three advantages that may make them attractive to high-volume production line builders: They have excellent handling characteristics, they can be cleaned up with water, and they can be painted over only 30 minutes after application (the cure continues after painting and is complete within 24 to 48 hours). In addition, acrylic latex sealants have good weather resistance and will adhere moderately well to fiber glass, aluminum, steel, and wood.

SILICONE SEALANTS

Most of us are familiar with silicone sealants and may even have used them in our bathrooms and kitchens. In general, they work well in places where they receive only light exposure to water and where the caulk is left alone—not touched, for example, by a scrub brush. In places where the sealant is continuously or frequently wet, the silicone usually must be replaced now and then. Moreover, wherever the silicone is used, that's what everyone sees—silicone—because it cannot be painted.

These same limitations apply to use of silicone sealant in the marine environment. As a result, silicone sealants are not widely recommended for use on the exterior of boats. Although these sealants adhere reasonably well to gel coat surfaces and metals, the silicone material itself is not particularly strong or tough. More importantly, because silicone sealants have relatively low moisture resistance, they should never be used below the waterline. They also are not recommended for use above the waterline where they will receive heavy exposure to water. Silicone sealants are not compatible with and should not be used with polypropylene plastics.

Additionally, silicone sealants should not be used for applications in which the sealant will be completely or almost completely cut off from air. The sealant contains a so-called "blocking agent" to prevent curing while it is in the tube. When the tube is opened and the sealant applied, the blocking agent evaporates into the air, allowing the material to cure. If the sealant is shut off from the air after it has been applied, the blocking agent may be prevented from evaporating and the sealant therefore prevented from curing.

There are two basic kinds of silicone sealants on the market today. The more common of the two uses an acid—usually acetic acid (hence the vinegar smell)—as the blocking agent. The less common variety uses an ammonia base. The practical difference between the two is that the acid-based sealant may have a corrosive effect on some metals whereas the ammonia-based sealant will not. In use, silicone sealants are difficult to clean up.

SILCONE / ACRYLIC SEALANTS

The development of a silicone / acrylic latex sealant for the marine industry represents an effort to combine the positive points of two separate rubber technologies into a single product that is superior to each of its components. The attempts appear to have been successful and these products are widely used.

The silicone / acrylic sealant combines the excellent adhesion of silicones and the relative toughness of the acrylic latex to provide a sealant that offers good, dynamic adhesive qualities. This sealant is suitable for bedding hatches, ports, windshields, and any deck hardware. The acrylic latex part of this technology makes other contributions as well. The silicone / acrylic sealant can be cleaned up with water, it is tough enough to be sanded, and it takes paint well. However, the silicone / acrylic product retains the one fundamental limitation common to both silicone and acylic sealants: It is not suitable for use below the waterline or elsewhere where it would be immersed in water continuously.

POLYSULFIDE SEALANTS

Polysulfide sealants are one of the workhorses of the marine industry. Polysulfide sealants have excellent adhesive properties and will adhere strongly to gel coat and wood. They are intended for use both above and below the waterline. They are relatively elastic, making them suitable for use in seams or joints that are subject to movement or flexing. They do not shrink when curing. They can be painted soon after application and sanded, if necessary, once they have fully cured. They also have good resistance to fuels and oil. There are, however, some limitations to their use. Although polysulfide sealants are compatible with most materials used in boat construction, they are not compatible with and should not be used with aluminum.

Polysulfide sealants normally take 7 to 10 days to achieve a full cure. The curing process uses moisture from the environment in the chemical reaction that takes place as the material sets up and cures. For that reason, the cure will be faster when the humidity is high than when it is low. The fastest cure, in fact, occurs when the polysulfide has been used below the waterline and the boat launched soon after.

The most common application for polysulfide sealants on fiber glass boats is sealing the seams between the planks of a teak deck. For a proper job, however, the teak should be treated with a primer that seals the natural oils into the wood before the polysulfide sealant is applied. These sealants also are used to bed hatches, through-hull fittings, ports, and deck fittings. Correctly applied, polysulfide sealants are expected to serve their function for 15 or more years.

POLYURETHANE SEALANTS

Polyurethane sealants are generally promoted as "adhesive / sealants." Indeed, the most widely used polyurethane sealant was originally developed to bond the layers of double-planked wood boat hulls. Today one of the most common applications for that same product is its use to seal hull-to-deck joints, in part because of the adhesive strength of the material and in part because the polyurethane sealant cures to a tougher, somewhat less flexible rubber than do, for example, the polysulfide sealants.

Polyurethane sealants are suitable for use either above or below the waterline. They too are moisture cured, drawing moisture from the environment to help form the links of the polymer chains that are created as the material cures. The polyurethanes tend to have very high internal strength so that the material itself holds together well. Often, in fact, the polyurethane sealant is stronger than one or more of the materials (e.g., wood) it is adhered to.

Like the polysulfides, the polyurethanes also have limitations. They are not recommended for use where they may be exposed to teak cleaners, because the solvents in many teak cleaners will attack the polyurethane rubber, making it revert to an uncured state. When that happens, the polyurethane sealant must be removed and replaced. When polyurethane sealants are used with teak, the builder must consult the directions for the particular product he is using. Depending upon the product being used, a primer may be recommended for use with teak.

There is still the mystery sealant, the product mentioned earlier whose chemistry is held as proprietary information by the manufacturer. This product reportedly was originally developed for the aircraft industry as a sealant and adhesive for such applications as sealing aircraft windows. It is said to be compatible with all materials used in boat construction, to be suitable for use either above or below the waterline, and to adhere more strongly than either polysulfides or polyurethane adhesive / sealants to gel coat surfaces and steel. The material is sold as a heavy-duty marine sealant. It contains a solvent as a blocking agent to prevent curing in the tube. Although the sealant skins over in 15 to 20 minutes after application as the solvent evaporates from the surface, a complete cure (i.e., complete evaporation of the solvent from all of the sealant) requires 3 to 7 days, depending upon the thickness of the sealant when it is applied. Because the solvent must be able to evaporate from the sealant for the cure to take place, the sealant should not be blocked off completely from the air before it has had ample cure time. Additionally, if used below the waterline, the sealant should be allowed to cure fully before the boat is launched. The sealant can be cleaned up with mineral spirits. No primer is needed when it is used with teak.

9

The Finished Boat
Surveying for Quality

Twenty-plus years ago, when fiber glass boats larger than open runabouts were first being built, it did not make much difference that few people knew enough about fiber-reinforced plastics to offer an informed opinion about how well a particular boat was constructed. At the time, most FRP boats were being built to wood boat scantlings (specifications). This translation of wood into FRP frequently resulted in boats with hulls so stout that some of their owners today describe them fondly as "icebreakers." By the mid-1970s, however, fiber glass-reinforced plastic was a familiar material. FRP scantlings were replacing wood scantlings and pleasure boats built like "icebreakers" were fast becoming an anachronism. Moreover, a set of "generally accepted good practices" had spread throughout the industry and a body of knowledge developed that enabled experts to offer opinion grounded in experience about the quality of construction of different FRP boats. More recently, as recounted throughout these pages, FRP technology has been expanding rapidly as demands for improved performance and lower production costs push the industry to try newer materials and construction systems. All of these changes have moved today's boats even farther from the "icebreaker" construction of the early 1960s. They have also made it increasingly difficult for amateurs to judge the quality of construction of many boats.

This change argues strongly for having a qualified marine surveyor make a thorough inspection of any boat—new or used—before completing a purchase agreement to ensure that the boat is sound. Although most people accept the notion that used boats need a survey to ensure everything is in good order, too few people recognize the same need when purchasing a new boat. The unfortunate fact, however, is that even new boats may have defects and those defects may be serious, ranging from missing hose clamps to voids in the laminate to a misshapen hull, the last the result of a hull being removed from the mold green and blocked up improperly. A qualified marine surveyor will pick up defects so they can be corrected before settlement or, if uncorrectable, so that a buyer does not get stuck with the marine version of a lemon.

Despite the need for a professional surveyor's services before a specific boat is purchased, there is much that amateurs can do for themselves when surveying the market to lessen the possibility of selecting a boat—new or used—that will ultimately turn out to be a lemon. If you have read this far, you already know more about boat construction than many if not most boat salesmen or yacht brokers. All that is needed is to apply what has been learned.

The key to any yacht survey—amateur or professional—is being methodical. It is too easy when going through a boat to notice only those factors that stand out, when in fact it may the smaller, less obtrusive elements which provide the best insight into the quality of worksmanship and materials that has gone into the boat. Moreover, a casual survey makes it difficult to compare one boat to another because you have not noticed the same or comparable elements in all of the boats. The obvious solution is preparation of a detailed survey list, a checklist that may run several pages if it allows sufficient room after each item for notes.

In developing the list, there are three factors to keep in mind. First, the checklist should progress from general elements to specific detail. Second, it should include separate sections for each area of the boat: for example, overall appearance, hull (exterior and interior); deck (exterior and interior), interior structural components; rigging (sailboats), engine installation, electical systems, and plumbing. Third, it should include items that help relate the boat being surveyed to the use intended for it. The following checklist illustrates one approach. This check-list is not all inclusive. It does include some design elements as well as construction-related items because of their importance to any survey activity. It does not include elements such as ade-quacy of construction specifications (lay-up schedule, rigging size, etc.), condition of equipment, and suitability of design and equipment that a professional surveyor would also consider.

OVERALL APPEARANCE

Out of the Water

• Just stepping back to look at the lines of the boat from a series of different vantage points, is it pretty? (I for one, am struck anew each time our boat is hauled at how pretty her lines are below the waterline as well as above.) The answer to this ques-tion says something about the aesthetic sense of the designer.

• To your eye, does the underwater portion of the boat appear proportional to the remainder of the boat above the waterline, considering not only the depth of the hull below the waterline, but also its breadth? The concern is that the boat not appear either top heavy or so massive below the waterline as to be pon-derous.

In the Water

• Stepping back from the boat, is it pretty when resting in the water? Does it look suited for the use you will make of it?

• If it is a sailboat, does its rig look the right size for the boat? Or does the mast look a bit short, perhaps suggesting not enough sail area for the boat?

• Does the boat rest on her marks? Or is she heavy in the bow or stern? Does she have a list to one side or the other?

THE HULL (OUT OF WATER)

• Are the two sides of the hull and its bottom symmetrical as viewed from fore and aft?

• Moving from bow to stern alongside the hull (on each side), does the fore and aft curvature of the hull topsides and bottom follow a smooth, graceful curve? Or are there bumps or dips that may suggest a misshapen hull?

• Looking at the gel coat, is it smooth and shiny? Are there blemishes, small spots where the color or surface texture is slightly different than the surrounding area, suggesting spot repair work on the gel coat? You can expect a few such areas, but very many is a flag.

• Looking along the sides of the hull, allowing light to reflect from the gel coat, are there faintly (or grossly) visible vertical lines that may show where a bulkhead or comparable reinforcement is attached to the inside of the hull? If so, that may reveal a hard spot that could be a source of trouble in years ahead. The location should be marked for comparison later to location of bulkheads or reinforcing points in a hull liner. (Note: Most structural problems with FRP boats occur at a joint of some kind, e.g., in the area of bulkheads, furniture attachments, windows, through-hulls, frames, hull-to-deck joints, etc.)

• If you push firmly on the side of the hull, particularly in the bow sections or any large flat sections, can you feel the hull panel move in and out? On a boat larger than about 20 feet, the acceptability of such a finding would depend greatly upon the use intended for the boat. In any case, such panel flexing is not a good sign.

• Does the boat have a separate rub rail? If not, does it depend upon the protruding edge of a toe rail or cap rail to serve as a rub rail?

• Does the boat have lines for the boot stripe (waterline) and, possibly, a cove stripe molded into the hull permanently?

• Does the boat have hard chines or round chines? Is the bottom rounded from chine to keel or more nearly flat? The hard chines promise a quicker rolling motion than round chines. The flat bottom sections also promise a quicker motion.

• Are through-hull fittings bronze, plastic, or simply FRP tubes through the bottom? Generally, bronze through-hulls are best practice. All holes through the hull that can be immersed in water under normal use (e.g., above the waterline on a sailboat, but immersed when heeling) should have some means of closing off the hole without having to resort to a wood plug. Bronze sea cocks are generally considered the preferred means of closure.

• Is there any sign that a core in the hull laminate has been compressed or crushed from tightening down on the through-hull or related fittings?

• On a powerboat, does the hull offer protection to propellers and rudders in the event of running aground?

• On a sailboat, does the boat have a full keel, high-aspect fin keel, or a moderate–aspect fin? If a full keel, does it sweep up along its leading edge right into the stem, or is it cut away in the front, providing a clean run of bottom for a few feet between the stem and the leading edge of the keel. In general, the cutaway forefoot promises better windward performance and easier tacking.

DECK EXTERIOR, INCLUDING HARDWARE

• Does the overall deck provide both a neat appearance and adequate space for line and anchor handling?

• Does the deck have a molded-in nonskid surface, a painted nonskid, or one of the plastic/cork composite nonskid surfaces? How effective does the nonskid appear?

• Are the side decks wide enough for safe passage forward? Are there adequate handholds for moving fore and aft when underway?

• Do the side decks, foredeck, and cabin top feel solid underfoot? Are there any creaking or cracking sounds when a heavy person walks along the deck? Such sounds may indicate delamination between the core and skin coats.

• If a sailboat, how large are windows or portlights? What material are fixed ports made of and how thick is it? How are fixed ports attached (e.g., an aluminum frame or bolted)? Are frames of opening ports made of plastic, aluminum, or bronze? Does the window portion of an opening port have a separate metal frame, or is the window made of plastic with integral dog ears?

• Are hatches flush with the deck or cabin house (in which case they are more likely to leak)?

• If the boat has a deck well for stowing an anchor and rode, does the well have a drain? (Sometimes builders forget that detail.) If so, is the outlet large enough to drain the well quickly, not be stopped up easily by pieces of grass, mud, or sand, and be cleared easily should it become plugged for any reason? Does the deck well have a gasket around the edge of its hatch to reduce the volume of water that seeps into the well when water gets on deck?

• Are mooring cleats, chocks, and other hardware positioned well for use? Does the boat have chocks amidships for spring lines?

• Wherever deck fittings are placed, is there any sign that the core has been crushed or compressed from tightening down on screws or bolts when installing the fitting?

• Are all windows, hatches, and hardware well bedded with a rubberlike sealant?

• Are bow and stern rails and any lifeline stanchions sturdy if you push firmly against them? Or do they feel flimsy? Are lifeline stanchions one piece with their bases, or can they be removed if necessary without removing the base? (Separate stanchions should be fastened in their bases with a machine screw through the wall of the base and threaded into the stanchion wall.)

• If a hole has been cut through the deck for a hatch, vent, or chain pipe, has the cut edge of the deck and any exposed core been sealed with resin or another long-lasting sealant? (If this cannot be determined from above deck, often the exposed edge of the hole can be seen from below.)

• Wherever bolt ends are exposed—where the bow rail is bolted to the pulpit, for example—has the builder used a flat washer (against wood or gel coat) and a lock washer under the nuts? Alternatively, has he used aircraft nuts (nuts with nylon inserts that prevent them from backing off accidently)? If the bolts do have nuts on them, have they been tightened firmly?

HULL AND DECK INTERIOR

• Wherever (and if) the final layer of the hull laminate is visible, does the fabric appear fully saturated with resin without swimming in it? The surface texture of the reinforcing fabric should be clearly visible to both sight and touch, but there should not be places where the resin clearly did not fill in the voids between fibers or bundles of fibers. Nor should there be so much resin that the surface is glassy smooth.

• Is the finish on the inner surface of the hull—and where it is visible on the underside of the deck—neat or somewhat sloppy?

• Is there easy access to all through-hull fittings? Do all through-hull fittings have backing plates? Do all through-hull fittings that might be immersed in water have closing devices, preferably sea cocks? Do other through-hull fittings also have closing devices? (Ideally, all would.)

• How is the rudderpost run through the hull? Through a tube extending from the hull bottom to a point above the waterline? Through a stuffing box? Is the area where the rudderpost goes through the hull reinforced in any manner? If so, to what extent? Is the rudderpost braced stoutly near deck level? How?

• If the hull and/or deck are cored, is the transition from cored area to solid FRP gradual (beveled) or sharp? Are all transitions you can find treated in the same manner? (The transition should be beveled.)

• Are the sides of the cabin house cored?

• How is the hull-to-deck joint made? What kind of fasteners are used? At what intervals? Is an excess of sealant visible to suggest no skimping on the quantity of sealant? What kind of sealant was used? Is there any sign of leakage?

• Is there easy access to the underside of all deck fittings, including toe rail fasteners, stanchion and pulpit bases, cleats, fill pipes, winches, and so on? Do all fittings that must withstand any external stresses have backing plates? What kind of fasteners are used? If bolts, have lock washers or aircraft nuts been used? (Note: Too often workers fail to put on or tighten all nuts, particularly in hard-to-reach places—even in the hull-to-deck joint!) Is there evidence of any sealant being used around the fasteners?

• If not visible from above, wherever holes have been cut in the deck—for example, around the chain pipe or ventilators—has the core in the deck laminate been sealed off? Or is the raw wood or foam visible?

• If the boat has a full hull liner, can you find in hanging lockers or other stowage compartments any place where the liner is mated to the hull (in lieu of a bulkhead, for example)? If so, how well does it fit? Is it bonded to the hull? How?

Interior Structural Components

• Does the boat have a reinforcing grid (stringers and frames) in the hull bottom? If so, how is it constructed? Does the construction appear sturdy? If wood is encapsuled in fiber glass materials, are there any gaps in the resin saturation that could allow bilge water to wet the wood, possibly causing problems of rot?
• Are any bulkheads or major furnishings located where vertical lines were noticed (if any were) in the gel coat during the earlier inspection from the ground?
• Are bulkheads bonded to the hull using fillet bonds? If not, does the edge of the bulkhead fit up against the hull? Or is there a gap between the hull and bulkhead edge? How far does the FRP tape extend onto the bulkhead? Onto the hull laminate? What kind of reinforcing fabric was used to tape the bulkhead to the hull? How many layers? If the bulkhead has a veneer, was that removed where the FRP tape adheres to the bulkhead? Are the bulkheads taped to the overhead? (Note: Even on boats made with full hull liners, there may be partial bulkheads beneath the cockpit that are visible from hatches to stowage areas, engines, and tanks.)
• How are interior components tied into the boat? Taped to the hull? Integral part of a hull liner? Combination of the two?
• Are corners of interior components rounded or sharp? Sharp corners are weapons in a seaway.

RIGGING (SAILBOATS)

• How are chain plates installed? If attached to knees, are they firmly fillet bonded to the hull? Is the bulkhead for chain plate attachment a minimum of ½ inch thick on boats under 30 feet, ¾ inch thick on boat from 30 to 40 feet, and thicker still on larger boats? (At least one production sailboat longer than 30-feet has used ¼-inch plywood for the bulkhead that anchors the upper shrouds, an inadequate arrangement.) Note: Some newer sailboats are using Navtec rods to tie shrouds into the reinforcing grid in the hull bottom, foregoing traditional chain plate attachment to bulkheads, knees, or to the hull itself. The suitability of this arrangement in a particular boat should be judged by a qualified surveyor.

ENGINE INSTALLATION

• Is there easy access to the engine for routine maintenance? If the engine fails, is there sufficient room to work on it in a seaway?
• Is the propeller shaft stuffing box easily accessible?
• Does the engine have an oil drip pan beneath it to prevent drippings from going into the bilge?
• Could the engine be removed if necessary without cutting holes in the deck or cabin?
• Is the fuel tank firmly fastened down so that it cannot move in rough water? Does the fuel system have a shutoff valve at the tank?

ELECTRICAL SYSTEMS

• Is all wiring neat? Are parallel wires bundled with plastic ties every 6 or 8 inches?
• Are wires color coded to help in tracing circuits?
• Are batteries installed so they cannot shift in a seaway? Does the battery box have a cover? Is the battery box ventilated?
• Do electrical systems (lights, etc.) all work?

PLUMBING SYSTEMS

• Are all tanks firmly fastened down?
• Do all hose ends, including those on engine systems, all

through-hull fittings, as well as sinks and heads, have two stainless steel hose clamps? (One is inadequate.)
• Is plumbing done neatly?
• Do water tanks have cleanout plates? Are tanks baffled? Can individual tanks be isolated from the system with their own shutoff valves?

As noted earlier, this kind of checklist omits a number of items a professional marine surveyor would look into, because specialized knowledge is necessary to evaluate what is found. It also assumes that builders are complying with federal safety requirements, but makes that assumption confident that any competent marine surveyor will focus heavily on safety. In the areas of rigging, engines, electrical systems, and plumbing, we have included only the most obvious elements and questions an amateur can answer. It is worth noting, however, that if a builder takes the trouble to run his wiring neatly, the odds are good he has also run it properly.

It should also be noted that modern practices in FRP boat construction often impose important limitations on anyone trying to evaluate quality of construction after a boat has already been built. For example, short of destructive testing, that is taking a core sample and burning the resin away to determine the glass-to-resin ratio and to see what reinforcing materials were used in the laminate, the manner in which FRP boats are finished makes it difficult to determine whether a hull or deck was molded properly.

Another example is that the use of hull and deck liners often makes it next to impossible to determine by direct observation how well a boat has been put together, because too much is covered up by the liners. And still another example, the emphasis today on engineering to remove weight by making hull lay-ups lighter and to provide compensating reinforcement by use of composite contruction, exotic materials, and structural grid or stringer systems is taking FRP construction away from its base of experience and putting it into an area of technology that few of us know enough about to make informed judgments.

All of this makes it increasingly important to visit the factory to see boats in various stages of completion to evaluate the quality of construction and attention to detail before making a commitment to a particular boat, a step any good boat builder will encourage. It also suggests consulting with a competent surveyor before making that commitment to a particular boat. If a new boat is being purchased, the cost of making an error may also suggest employing an agent to follow the boat of choice right on through construction to make sure it is constructed as represented by the builder. There are two ways to do this. One is to employ the services of either Lloyds Registry of Shipping or the American Bureau of Shipping. Both institutions are set up to oversee the construction of boats to ensure they are built to specifications approved by them. However, few U.S. builders of production boats are willing to go to the trouble or expense of offering either a Lloyds or an American Bureau of Shipping certificate with their boats.

The alternative to Lloyds or the American Bureau of Shipping is for boat buyers to employ the services of a competent marine surveyor to inspect the boat one or more times during construction, before the boat leaves the factory, and after the boat has been delivered for commissioning to be certain it was not damaged in transit.

FINDING A GOOD SURVEYOR

One should not assume that everyone who calls himself or herself a marine surveyor is competent. Or that he is competent to survey an FRP boat. It is not much of an overstatement to say that virtually anyone can hang out a shingle that proclaims he is a marine surveyor. There are generally no licensing requirements. Moreover, there are excellent surveyors whose expertise is large ships or steel or aluminum motor yachts rather than modern FRP power or sailing yachts. What this means, of course, is that anyone who wants to employ a marine surveyor competent to survey his boat may have to put in a little effort to find one.

A good marine surveyor brings much more than knowledge

of proper boat building practices to the job. He is an experienced seaman who knows what the ocean has to offer. As a result, he is able to comment knowledgeably on the suitability of a boat for the use the buyer intends for it. He also has gained knowledge over the years about a wide range of builders and their boats. Therefore he is likely to know the idiosyncracies of many boats and where problems tend to arise. It should be noted also that some surveyors tend to specialize in sailboats or powerboats.

There are several ways to find a good surveyor. One common approach is to ask other boat owners if they know of a good surveyor. In this way, you have the advantage of finding out whether those people were satisfied with the job their surveyors did for them. Some boat owners may even be willing to let you see their survey reports so that you can evaluate the surveyor's apparent thoroughness (if not the validity of his comments). In addition, most yacht brokers keep a list of surveyors they have found competent to work with their clients; large, reputable brokers cannot afford to deal with incompetent surveyors. Other sources of referrals include insurance companies and the National Association of Marine Surveyors in New York, which can provide the names of its members in different areas of the country who are qualified to survey FRP yachts.

10

Maintenance
A Little Work Each Day
Keeps Problems Away

The greatest myth about fiber glass is that it is maintenance free. True, a person can purchase a boat and not touch the hull except to apply bottom paint, or the deck except to walk on it, and the boat will not fall apart as a result. It will, however, begin to look a bit dingy after a couple of years as the ultraviolet rays in the sunlight degrade the surface of the gel coat, paling colors and creating a chalky surface. If the gel coat is cracked or chipped down to the laminate, as almost inevitably happens through normal use, moisture may gradually work its way into the laminate, wicking along any glass fibers exposed by the chip or crack in the gel coat. Although the moisture will not hurt the laminate itself, it may cause difficulty over a period of years if it reaches a wood core, soaks into the wood, and thereby weakens the structure. How far such moisture might spread into the core would depend upon a variety of factors, including whether the core were plywood or end-grain balsa. If any such moisture were to pool in a void—where the core did not adhere properly to the outer skin, for example—and then freeze during winter, the expanding ice formed might gradually turn a void into a growing area of delamination.

It is difficult, of course, to describe any such potential problems without risk of overstating the likelihood of their arising.

The potential of such problems occurring, however, is real, and that's the bad news. The good news is that very little effort is needed to prevent such problems. A relatively small amount of ongoing maintenance will keep the boat's original gel coat looking good and serving as an effective moisture barrier for at least 5 years and often 10 or more, depending upon the quality of the gel coat resin and the care used in its application during the boat's construction.

Maintenance for a boat's gel coat above the waterline falls into three basic areas: keeping the gel coat clean; keeping it shiny; and repairing any chips, scratches, dings, and cracks that may develop. Eventually, of course, even a well-maintained gel coat needs added help if the boat is to continue looking its best. That added help usually comes in a paint can. Below the waterline, the predominant maintenance problem is blistering of the gel coat, but here too various scratches and gouges may need repair if the boat has been run aground or run into heavy debris while underway.

KEEPING THE GEL COAT CLEAN

The gel coat of a boat is essentially a thick polyester paint. It provides a tough, hard surface. Because it has been applied against a highly polished mold, a new boat's gel coat also presents a very smooth, shiny surface. That shine, of course, has an aesthetic value, but it is also utilitarian: The shiny smoothness makes it easier to keep the boat clean because it provides little footing for dirt or algae.

The goal of any gel coat maintenance program is to maintain that hard, smooth surface finish to the extent possible. As a result, the first part of gel coat maintenance involves hosing down the hull and deck surfaces regularly to wash off dust, grit, sand, or other abrasive matter that may collect on the boat's exterior surfaces and be rubbed against the gel coat, scratching the smooth surface. It is obvious, of course, that such abrasive dirt on a deck may be ground underfoot. Dirt on the hull topsides may also be ground against the gel coat—under a fender, for example, as it is rubbed against the hull while doing its job.

All such grinding of grit against the gel coat gradually degrades the smooth surface finish.

The second part of gel coat maintenance involves cleaning up stains. These may result from spilled liquids, oily harbor water, organic matter in river or bay water, or any number of other sources, including steel tools or cans left on deck where they can get wet and leave behind a spot of rust.

There is a right way and a wrong way to attack stains on a gel coat surface. The wrong way involves the use of abrasive cleansers. In general, one should not use a household cleanser to remove stains or dirt from a gel coat surface, because such cleansers scratch the gel coat. As implied earlier, dirt and stains will accumulate much more readily on a scratched surface than they will on a smooth gel coat surface.

The "right way" to attack gel coat stains involves following a series of steps that progresses from the mildest to the "harshest" alternatives, none of which even approaches the harshness of household cleansers. The first step is rubbing the stained area with a soft rag soaked with a readily available solvent such as the alcohol, kerosene, or diesel fuel used as a stove or engine fuel on the boat. These fuels will dissolve many stains without attacking the gel coat. There are, of course, many other solvents that can be used to clean up stains on fiber glass. Most, however, are expensive. More importantly, most of these other solvents are not safe to keep on a boat routinely either because they are highly flammable or toxic or both.

If one of the "fuel" solvents will not remove the stain, alternatives include using a commercial stain remover sold in a marine store, a wax/cleaner, or an automotive rubbing compound. Generally, commercial stain removers are formulated to react chemically with the stain, making it disappear. One such product, a gel that is brushed onto a small area of the hull or deck and then washed off with a hose, is effective in removing brown waterline stains, exhaust residue, and rust stains from white gel coat. There are also rust stain removers readily available in marine stores. A word of caution, however, before using a stain remover on anything other than a white gel coat: The stain remover should be tested on a hidden area to be certain it will not bleach the pigment in the gel coat.

If a commercial stain remover will not do the job, is unsuitable, or is not readily available, the next alternative is to use a wax that does double duty as a cleaner. Such waxes contain a mild abrasive and a solvent system that may be sufficient to remove the stain. If the wax/cleaner does not work, the next step is to use an automotive rubbing compound. A white rubbing compound is recommended because it is much less abrasive than the red compound commonly used in automotive finishing shops. A thin coating of the pastelike rubbing compound is spread over the stain using a soft cloth, and then rubbed with lots of elbow grease using a soft cheesecloth. The rubbing compound will eventually clean up the stain by wearing away the affected surface layer of gel coat. A less desirable but still acceptable alternative is to use one of the new liquid soft scrubbing cleaners developed for use in our homes on fiber glass shower stalls and bathtubs. While these contain an abrasive, it is relatively soft and will cause minimal scratching if used judiciously. Advantages of both a rubbing compound and the liquid scrubbing cleaner are that they are relatively inexpensive, safe to use, and can be stowed safely for long periods on a boat.

KEEPING THE GEL COAT SHINY

The most insidious threat to gel coat is weathering, particularly the degradation caused by the ultraviolet (UV) rays that are part of our normal sunlight. Understanding what happens in the weathering process requires recalling that gel coat is a polyester resin mixed with mineral fillers and, usually, a pigment to give it color. In the weathering process, the UV rays break down the resin on the surface of the gel coat, leaving behind only the chalklike pigment and fillers. The process is relatively slow, but, as a walk around any marina with a number of older boats will demonstrate, it is inevitable.

Short of painting the boat, there is no way to provide absolute protection for the gel coat against UV attack. It is possible, however, to give the elements something to chew on before they get to the gel coat, and that is the function of wax. Just how much protection wax offers is subject to debate. Experts consulted for this book generally believe that waxing a boat's gel coat will help slow the normal weathering process, but they do not really know so for a fact. In any case, that protection is almost certainly less than the advertisements for your favorite wax claim and it may be only cosmetic—cleaning off the slightly weathered surface each time the boat is waxed so that, although the gel coat is being gradually worn down by the weathering–waxing sequence, it is kept looking good as it wears.

Traditionally, carnauba waxes have been considered among the best available. Carnauba is a natural wax derived from the carnauba palm leaf. Over the past 10 years, however, advances in silicone polymer chemistry have made carnauba wax obsolete. Today even in a wax consisting of a blend of carnauba and silicone, it is the silicone, not the carnauba, that remains on the hull to give it a slick, shiny coat. The carnauba acts mainly as a carrier.

Some waxes today also contain a UV screen that is said to help shield the gel coat from the damaging effects of UV rays. Two facts should be understood. Such waxes probably do contain a substance that can screen out UV rays; however, the wax layer is so thin—on the order of 20 microns (about eight tenthousandths of an inch)—that the UV screen is of little or no real benefit.

Many products sold today are labeled "cleaners" as well as waxes and are formulated to clean and wax the surface in one operation. As noted earlier, most of these formulations include an abrasive that cleans the surface by a mild grinding action similar to the action of a metal polish on silver or brass. Waxes that are called polishes (as opposed to cleaners) are likely to have a higher abrasive content.

An alternative to wax with an abrasive cleaner is one that works by a solvent action. These wax/cleaners are specifically advertised as having no abrasives. One such product is said by its manufacturer to work by penetrating through the dirt and chalky gel coat surface and then lifting them from the good gel coat to be removed by the rubbing action as the wax is polished.

When waxing a boat, of course, there are a number of practical considerations. For example, what parts of the boat should be waxed? How often should the boat be waxed? And are two coats better than one?

Every gel coat surface except where people will be walking can be waxed. The reason for not waxing walking surfaces, that is, decks, is very simply one of safety. Silicone waxes, in particular, create very slippery surfaces and may make deck surfaces hazardous even when people are wearing boat shoes. In essence, this limits the use of waxes to vertical surfaces or hardtops not intended as traffic areas. The irony, of course, is that horizontal (walking) surfaces receive the most direct exposure to sunlight and are therefore most vulnerable to UV degradation. In general, however, the action of walking on the decks and scrubbing decks to keep them clean helps keep the gel coat surface in good condition.

How often a boat should be waxed depends a great deal on where it is used and where it is kept. For example, a boat used in Maine or Puget Sound receives much less exposure to solar UV radiation than one kept in Key West or San Diego. Similarly, a boat kept under a shed receives considerably less UV exposure than one kept on a mooring. Leaving those extremes aside, however, and assuming some "average" exposure to sunlight, the boat should be waxed at least twice each year, and probably three times: once during spring fitting out, once midway through the summer, and once again in the late autumn. One word of caution: The "shine" on your hull is not a good guide as to whether the boat needs a new coat of wax. If the gel coat is in reasonable condition, that shine persists for months after the wax has worn off.

Whether two coats of wax are better than one depends on the definition of *better*. Today's silicone waxes are formulated to adhere to the gel coat, not to themselves. This means that a second coating of wax does not result in an appreciably thicker coating of wax. However, the second coating may pick up where the first left off in cleaning and smoothing the surface, with the result that the gel coat may look cleaner and shine more after the second coat. So there may be a slight cosmetic benefit initially, but the coat of wax will not last any longer.

In addition to waxes, there are so-called polymer coatings on the market that are claimed to offer protection against weathering for extended periods with only a light renewal coating every 6 months. These products are not recommended for use on gel coats that have been severely weathered, because they do not have the cleaning capability of combination waxes and cleaners. They are promoted instead for use on new boats or boats whose gel coat has been restored to good condition. If these coatings perform as advertised, their principal advantage is that their use may reduce frequency of waxing. Although they are claimed to greatly reduce weathering or chalking, the claim is difficult to test because the product is being used on a new gel coat or one already in good condition, both of which would probably not show signs of weathering for many months with normal care.

REPAIRING SCRATCHES, CRACKS, DINGS, CHIPS, AND GOUGES

One advantage to waxing a boat routinely is that it forces boat owners to pay attention to the gel coat surface. As a result, although scratches and dings may go unnoticed as they occur, they will stand right out when the hull and cabin house are being waxed. The important next step, of course, is to repair even minor dings or scratches when they are found. Such repairs can be done easily as a part of routine maintenance. However, it is important to remove all wax from the area being repaired or the patch may not adhere to the gel coat.

There are a variety of polyester and epoxy puttys that can be used to repair damaged gel coat, including some one-part gel coat repair products which come in a tube and are simply squirted into the scratch or crack. Generally, one-part gel coat repair products should be considered only a temporary remedy. Usually, the one-part products are cured by exposure to the air or sun; there is no chemical cross-linking. As a result, they are likely to dry out, shrink, or crack within a year or so and then need replacing.

Repair putties or pastes that require mixing two parts or addition of a hardener, on the other hand, are cured by chemical cross-linking. The cross-linking not only forms a tough internal structure within the repair putty itself, but also helps bond the putty to both the surrounding gel coat and the exposed underlying laminate. In general, polyester putties are less expensive and cure more quickly than epoxy putties. However, polyester resins must be shielded from air to cure. This means covering the patch with a piece of plastic film—Saran Wrap, for example—or sprayed with polyvinyl alcohol to obtain a cure. Though more expensive, epoxy putties will bond more strongly to the damaged area and shrink less when curing. If the gel coat is other than white, repair putties must be pigmented to match the gel coat color; some putties must be pigmented for use even with a white gel coat. The acrylic pigments used to color paints used in auto body shops work well with gel coat; usually only a few drops of pigment are needed.

Scratches

Scratches come in two degrees of severity. Surface scratches that mar but do not gouge the gel coat deeply are best handled by using an automotive rubbing compound to buff them out, either by hand or by using an electric drill with a buffing pad at low speed.

Deeper scratches need to be filled; they may also need to be deepened slightly to provide a good holding surface for the repair putty. The corner of a paint scraper or the point of a can opener (the old church key variety) often can be used effectively to enlarge a scratch; a better device is a small, high-speed power tool called a Moto tool. It resembles a small hand drill, but operates at very high speed using small bits reminiscent of dental drill bits. Alternatively, burr bits available for standard electric drills can be used, though not as easily. Using a small, pointed bit, a steady hand can enlarge a scratch just enough to ensure a good bonding surface for the repair putty. Before applying the repair putty, the enlarged scratch should be cleaned with lacquer thinner or acetone to be certain all wax is removed. It is useful also to blow out the scratch using compressed air, for example, from a can of Dust Off sold in photo supply stores for blowing dust off negatives in the darkroom

(Fig. 22). The repair putty, pigmented to match the gel coat as closely as possible, should be worked into the crevice formed by the cleaned out scratch, and any excess removed from the surrounding gel coat. When the putty is completely cured, the patch can be wet-sanded lightly with a very fine wet and dry paper and then buffed with a rubbing compound.

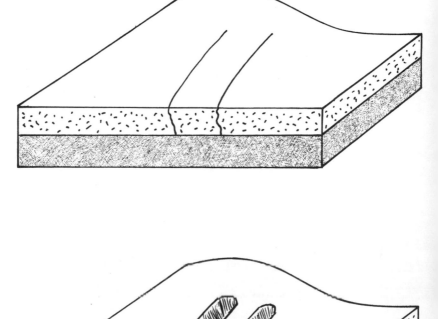

FIG. 22. Hairline cracks in gel coat should be enlarged slightly, preferably using a fine V-shaped burr bit in an electric drill or high-speed Moto tool.

Cracks or Crazing

At first glance, such minor cracks in the gel coat surface may seem too minor to be concerned about. However, not only should they be repaired, they should also be considered a possible sign of a more serious problem. For example, if cracks occur down the topsides opposite an interior structure, that cracking or crazing may well be a warning that the interior structure is causing a hard spot in the hull and that the hull panel is flexing over the hard spot. At the least, the situation probably calls for a professional diagnosis. The hull may need stringers added to stop the flexing. In addition, the joint between the interior structure and the hull may also need modification.

If one assumes that any surface cracks or crazing in the gel coat are superficial, repairs still should be made promptly to prevent them from becoming future problems. In general, the same approach used for deep scratches works well when repairing cracks or crazing. The important point is to provide an adequate groove to ensure a good bond for the repair putty. Because it is almost impossible to achieve a perfect color match between the repair putty and gel coat, care should be used to avoid making the scratches or cracks any larger than necessary.

Dings and Chips

Dings usually are the result of banging the gel coat into something, a dock, for example. A chip may result from dropping a tool onto the deck or cabin house. A chip may also result when the gel coat covering a void in the skin coat breaks away. Such voids occur when the first layer of fiber glass mat is not wet out or rolled out adequately when it is applied against gel coat in the mold. Eventually, the gel coat over such voids "chips" away, leaving the underlying layer of FRP mat exposed to the elements. Usually, the area involved is not much larger than a quarter.

Dings and chips usually do not need enlarging; however, it is good practice to pry gently around the edge to be sure the surrounding gel coat is not ready to break off. If the chip resulted from a void beneath the gel coat, it is worthwhile to tap gently around the area to test for the presence or absence of other voids. It is not uncommon for there to be more than one void in the same area.

Because repair putty often shrinks as it cures and the area being filled is large enough for such shrinkage to be visible, it is useful to put a strip of masking tape around the edge of the damaged area and to overfill the wound to the height of the masking tape, using a putty knife to smooth the top of the putty. In this way, the patch will not shrink below the surface of the gel coat. When the patch has been wet-sanded down to the level of the gel coat using first a 400 and next a 600 grit wet or dry paper, and then compounded, it will blend right into the gel coat surface.

Gouges

The only difference between repairing gouges and chips or dings is the size of the wound. The larger size and the often greater depth of gouges generally makes it even more important to overfill the wound (Fig. 23). It is far easier to wet-sand an excess of repair putty down to the level of the gel coat than it is to fill in an area where the putty has shrunk to create a low spot. If excessive shrinkage does occur, it may be best to grind the wound out partially and fill it a second time. Usually, however, filling to the height of masking tape placed alongside the gouge will provide the margin of excess needed. If gouges are on a vertical surface and are large or deep enough, it may be necessary to fill them in two stages to prevent the putty from sagging.

RESTORING A BOAT'S SURFACE FINISH

No matter how carefully one cares for a boat's gel coat, the finish will not last forever. After 5 or perhaps up to 10 years,

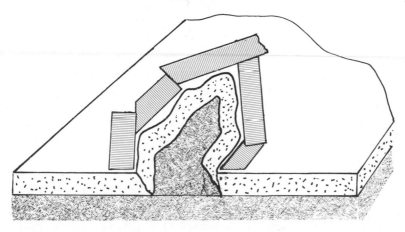

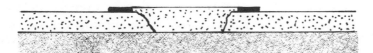

Fig. 23. When the gel coat has been dinged or gouged, the damaged area should be ground out carefully down to the skin coat. The edges of the opening should be taped with a single layer of masking tape and the damaged area filled with repair putty to the top of the masking tape. After the putty has cured and the masking tape has been removed, the repair patch can be faired into the surrounding gel coat with very fine wet or dry sandpaper and rubbing compound.

the only practical way to restore the boat's original surface beauty and to provide continued protection to the laminate against moisture is to paint the gel coat.

The technology of paints, like that of FRP, has moved rapidly in recent years. As a result, the paints on the market today are better than ever before. However, there are only three basic types of paint commonly used for an FRP boat's topsides: alkyd-(oil) based paints, modified alkyds, and two-part polyurethane coatings.

Alkyd Paints

These oil-based paints are the basic marine paints boat own-ers have used for years. The paint will look good for about a year. After several years of repeated applications, the paint must be removed, because the buildup becomes excessively thick. The principal advantage of these paints is price. They are generally less expensive than the other two types. They are also easy to use, easy to clean up, and relatively nontoxic.

Modified Alkyd Paints

These are ordinary oil-based paints that have had an epoxy or polyurethane component added to them. They are one-part products that go on and clean up just like ordinary alkyd paints. They do not require mixing two components or adding a catalyst. Though their brand names may sound like "epoxy" or "ure-thane"—even containing the words—they should not be con-fused with either an epoxy resin or one of the new two-part polyurethane coatings. With those caveats, the modified alkyd paints are generally more durable, offering, according to man-ufacturers, perhaps a 50 percent or more longer lifetime than conventional alkyd paints. They are also somewhat more expensive.

Two-Part Polyurethane Coatings

The difference begins with the nomenclature. These prod-ucts are properly called coatings, not paints. The two-part polyurethanes were used initially in the aircraft industry, where any paint not only must be tough and glossy, but must also withstand assault by a variety of oils and solvents. The products now sold in the marine market bring these same attributes to their use on boats.

The essential difference between a two-part polyurethane and ordinary paint lies in the way they cure. Whereas alkyd paints cure by evaporation to leave a film on the surface, a two-part polyurethane coating forms a film over the surface by a cross-linking process that relies upon moisture in the air. One way to envision what takes place as these finishes cure is to imagine a series of long ropes stretched out parallel to each other along the ground. If you use a number of short lines to tie the longer pieces together to make a cargo net, you are forming the cross-links. In polyurethane paints, these cross-links are formed by a reaction between the moisture in the air, a group of chemicals called isocyanates strung along one "rope," and hydrogen spotted along the resin base forming a parallel "rope." In brushing or spraying the polyurethane coating onto your topsides, you are laying out the long parallel ropes. As the chemical reaction by which the coating cures takes place, moisture is absorbed from the air to form the cross-links that build the cargo net of protection over your boat.

The remarkable features of the two-part polyurethane coatings are their mirrorlike gloss, depth of color, and durability. With good surface preparations and proper application, these coatings will make most boats look better than they did when new. Moreover, under normal usage the finish should last several years without renewing because of the superior abrasion resistance, chemical resistance, and color and gloss retention of these coatings. Nor will the finish require significant maintenance. The only routine care recommended is washing the surface down with fresh water and, occasionally, a detergent. If more stubborn dirt clings to the surface, alcohol and normal paint thinners may be used without endangering the finish.

There are, of course, differences between the various two-part polyurethanes on the market. From a practical viewpoint, however, the most important consideration is which product the person who will paint your boat is accustomed to using. If you are going to do it yourself, the question then becomes, Which product have people in your boatyard used with good results? Once you have settled on a product, it is important to follow carefully the manufacturer's instructions.

There are three key steps in the use of any two-part polyurethane coating. First is removal of any and all wax that may be on the gel coat. If the wax is not completely removed, the finished job will be marred by "fish eyes" where the film has not bonded properly to the gel coat because of the wax. Today, since most marine waxes contain silicone in one form or another, the best bet is to obtain a silicone wax stripper from an automobile paint shop. Silicones are difficult to remove and will not be removed reliably by ordinary wax removers or solvents. When removing the wax, you should plan on using a large number of rags, changing rags frequently to avoid simply spreading the wax around. The rags should be wet thoroughly with the stripper.

The second step is surface preparation. The extraordinarily high gloss of the two-part polyurethane finish will reveal even small imperfections in the surface. As a result, the care in fairing the gel coat surface will have major impact on the quality of the finished coating. If the work is done professionally, about 60 percent of the cost of the job is for surface preparation. This means finding and filling all scratches, dings, and so on, and then wet-sanding the repairs to obtain a smooth surface. If there is even a small edge along a repair, though barely discernible in the gel coat, it will be clearly evident in the mirror finish of the two-part polyurethane coating.

The third step is application of the coating itself. Two coats are required. The first coating generally does not look very good because the film is very thin. The second coating provides a miracle. Some professionals apply a third coating of a clear finish to add still more depth to the finish.

Many professionals use a spray gun to apply these coatings. The spray system must be "airless," however, because moisture in the compressed air will interfere with the application. In addition, because the strong solvents required for the sprayable products are toxic, the spray gun operator should wear a mask feeding him a fresh air supply. Some yard operators do not like the strong solvent systems required for the sprayable products and offer a brush-on system instead.

Two-part polyurethane coatings sold for use by nonprofessionals all are formulated to be applied with a brush. These systems also contain strong solvents and should be used only with good ventilation or outdoors. In general, it should be noted that two-part polyurethanes for spray application probably provide a slightly tougher finish and have a depth of gloss that experts, at least, will argue is better than that achieved with a brushable product. Some would argue that the difference in appearance is in the eyes of the beholder, not in the finish itself.

Anyone who has not used a two-part polyurethane before is well advised to tackle a small project before trying to apply one of these products to his boat. The small project might be a dinghy—yours or a friend's. As one who did not take that advice, let me describe the problems.

As noted earlier, the two-part polyurethanes are moisture cured. The full cure takes about a week. The cure also is affected by temperature. Ideal conditions would be about 60 percent relative humidity and about 70° F. If the humidity is below about 50 percent, the finish will not cure properly, and possibly not at all. The higher the humidity, the faster the coating cures. Similarly, the temperature should be at least 65° F. If it drops too much overnight before the cure is complete, the coating may never cure and may have to be removed for a whole new start. Higher temperatures and direct sunlight speed up the cure. Moreover, although these finishes use moisture for the curing process, they do not like water until after at least the outer surface is well cured. The surface must be dry before application and even a light dew at night before the finish has cured adequately will damage the finish.

For the professional who is working indoors, these conditions present no problem. He can control his environment. The amateur, probably working outdoors, however, has to accept the conditions nature serves up. What this generally means is that the work is done far enough into the day to be hotter than ideal and far enough into the warm weather so that humidity is higher than one would prefer. The result is that the paint sets up so quickly that one person usually cannot expect to do the job himself on a boat larger than about 20 feet or the finish will be characterized by brush strokes. Even a 20-footer with a high freeboard might be too much for a single person.

The solution is not difficult, but it does involve good teamwork with three or possibly four people working together, one applying the coating with a top-quality, short-nap roller; another one or two, depending upon the boat's freeboard, following behind with badger hair brushes, lightly brushing out the bubbles left by the roller; and the last ready to hand the person with the roller a fresh pot of the "paint" when needed so that there is no break in the application process until the entire job is completed. In addition, the helpers with the brushes must keep up with the roller. The coating may begin to set up within as little as 3 or 4 minutes after it has been rolled onto the hull or deck surface. Although the paint in the pot does not set up as quickly, the pot life is short. As a result, only as much as can be applied in 10 minutes or so should be mixed up at one time. An extender can be added to the "paint" to give a slightly longer working time, but it should be used with caution, following directions explicitly.

Once the step of painting an FRP boat is taken, of course, the painted coating becomes the new moisture barrier for the laminate. By this time, part of the gel coat has been worn away by the continued sequence of UV degradation and waxing. In addition, another part has been sanded away when preparing the surface for the new paint. As a result, even the painted surface must be maintained. Although the two-part polyurethanes are surprisingly abrasion resistant, they are not immune to damage. For that reason, prompt attention to possible damage to this coating is also recommended. Some scratches may be touched up with a brush. Larger scrapes normally are best touched up with a spray gun if an airless gun is available, because the repair can be feathered onto the undamaged surface. Caution is suggested before attempting to buff or compound a repair to blend the newly painted area into the old. Some of the two-part polyurethanes should not be buffed or compounded. Consulting the directions that come with the "paint" is recommended.

GEL COAT BLISTERS

One problem that has persisted with FRP boats over the years has been the formation of blisters in the gel coat below the waterline. The problem is so commonplace that some experts claim the odds are good that any boat in the water on a continuing basis (for a season, as opposed to being taken in and out on a trailer, for example) will eventually have some degree of a blister problem.

There has been an impressive amount of research into the cause and prevention of gel coat blisters. The cause appears to be related to migration of water through the gel coat to the laminate. Some people believe the blisters are caused by a reaction between the water that migrates through the gel coat and undissolved binders or unreacted catalyst which may remain on exposed fiber ends if the skin coat was not wet out thoroughly. The addition of extenders or other additives to the gel coat resin at the boat factory before the gel coat is sprayed into the mold may also affect formation of blisters. In general, however, three basic elements are thought to influence formation of gel coat blisters: gel coat thickness, resin quality, and the boat's exposure to water.

As noted in Chapter 2, polyester resins come in a wide variety of formulations. Commonly, however, the choice of two specific components plays an important role in determining a resin's water resistance. One is the choice of saturated acid; the other is the choice of glycols. In general, a gel coat made with isophthalic acid and neopentyl glycol (NPG) has greater water resistance than other gel coat resins. Both isophthalic acid and NPG add to the cost of the resin.

In general, the thicker the gel coat, the better its water resistance as well. There are limits, however. Too thick an application is more vulnerable to cracking and chipping, failures that may cause water migration problems of a different type. Too thin an application, on the other hand, is excessively susceptible to blistering. The recommended minimum thickness for gel coat is 16 to 20 mils; the optimum thickness is from 20 to 22 mils.

A boat normally kept on a trailer and put in the water only for periods of immediate use is unlikely to develop a blister problem. At the other extreme, a boat kept in the water year round in the subtropical environment of southern Florida is almost assured the problem. Hauling the boat periodically allows moisture that has gathered behind the gel coat to escape, inhibiting blister formation. However, even boats that spend 6 months in the water and 6 months out often suffer blisters.

Depending upon the severity of the problem, gel coat blisters may result in anything from a minor maintenance chore to a time-consuming and tedious repair job. In both cases, however, the treatment of choice is the same. The gel coat must be ground or sanded away from around each blister, the excavation filled with a repair putty (preferably an epoxy putty), and the patch faired into the remaining gel coat. If the problem has been extensive, or appears to be progressing in that direction, one can consider also removing all traces of bottom paint, rough-sanding the entire area below the waterline, and applying a coating of a pigmented two-part epoxy marine laminating resin over the gel coat as a kind of waterproofing layer. Bottom paint can then be applied over the epoxy resin. In using all of these materials, of course, it is important to read and follow the manufacturers' instructions and to heed any recommended precautions.

11

Repairs with FRP
Plastic Surgery with Good Results

A well-constructed fiber-reinforced plastic boat is a remarkably strong and durable product. With reasonable care, it will last many years. At any time, however, carelessness, bad luck, misuse, inadequate design or construction, or some combination of these may result in more than the surface damage described in Chapter 10. When that happens, one discovers still another advantage offered by FRP construction: the relative ease with which even serious damage can be repaired.

Some years ago, for example, when I was looking for a boat I could use for weekending with the family, the manager of a local marina offered to sell me a 6-month-old but severely battered 26-foot sloop he had bought in a salvage sale from an insurance company. He explained that his yard could make all necessary repairs and promised I would end up with a better-than-new boat for less than the new boat price. The yard had an excellent reputation; the price was just within my means; and I knew the type of boat well enough to know it offered what I was looking for. As a result, I agreed to look at the boat and discuss the work that would be done in more detail.

Fortunately, I was about 98 percent determined to accept the offer before I saw the boat. It was not in any condition to instill much confidence in its future. I could well understand why the insurance company had totaled it. The boat had dragged anchor up against a steel dock at night during a severe October storm and had lain wave and windblown against the dock for hours, abrading away the fiber glass along the hull-to-deck joint, banging severely enough to break a crack through the hull and eventually sink her. When I saw the boat on a trailer, she had about 6 inches of hull and 2 inches or more of deck worn away along her port side for more than half the length of the boat. On the starboard side, many of the pop rivets fastening the hull-to-deck joint had come loose, opening up that joint. The interior was a shambles of mud and still soggy cushions. Chain plates for the port shrouds were missing and the rigging ruined.

To make a long story short, I bought the boat on faith and the yard manager's reputation. When I took delivery of the repaired boat about a month later—for about 10 percent below the new boat price—she was beautiful. The crack in the hull was repaired. The long hole worn along the hull and deck joint was repaired. Elsewhere, the entire hull-to-deck joint had been refastened and then covered over with an FRP bond that began well inboard along the deck and which was carried 6 inches down the sides of the hull. The patch had been faired beautifully into the hull and deck and the boat sprayed with Awlgrip, a two-part polyurethane coating. The interior was clean and bright. I had new rigging that was heavier than the original and a new engine. She was indeed a better-than-new boat and we enjoyed her for two seasons before selling her very quickly for a good price.

Considerably more dramatic testimony to the repairability of FRP construction is told by world sailor Hal Roth in his book *Two Against Cape Horn*. Roth and his wife, Margaret, along with two companions were shipwrecked in the Roth's 35-foot FRP sloop, *Whisper,* just 24 miles from Isla Hornos, the island whose southern face is better known as Cape Horn. By the time of their rescue and the subsequent salvage of *Whisper,* days of pounding on the rocks had created what Roth described in the book as "an evil-looking U-shaped tear that measured forty-seven inches long in a horizontal direction. At the forward end, the tear turned vertically upward for eight inches. At the after end, the tear rose nearly twenty six inches" (p. 209). The damage to *Whisper's* starboard side, Roth said, "was serious, but after pounding at each high tide for eleven days it was surprising that the problems weren't worse. The resiliency and strength of the fiberglass hull were remarkable" (p. 220).

Working in a navy shipyard in Southern Chile, the Roths were allowed 3 weeks to repair their hull, which, when the damaged area was cut away, had a hole about 70 inches long and 35 inches high in the port side. With the help of workers at the yard, they met that deadline and subsequently completed their voyage around Cape Horn.

Most repairs, of course, are neither so dramatic nor so extensive as those required by *Whisper*. But the Roths used repair material and techniques similar to those used in any yard to repair an FRP boat. The basic procedures are relatively simple. The job, however, may be more complex, depending upon the size of the damaged area and whether the laminate is solid FRP or cored, whether a hull or deck liner has been used, and whether any interior reinforcing members such as bulkheads, stringers, and frames are involved.

In general, for small repairs, chopped strand mat and fiber glass boat cloth are the reinforcing fabrics of choice. Using a ¾- or 1-ounce mat in alternating layers with the boat cloth makes it easier to obtain a good glass-to-resin ratio; the disadvantage is that more layers are required because the lighter mat and the boat cloth are relatively thin. For larger areas, 18- or 24-ounce woven roving and 1.5 ounce mat should be used—with one exception. If an exotic fabric such as unidirectional roving or a fabric of Kevlar was used in the original lay-up, that same fabric should be used for all but very small repairs. In such an instance, the repair is best done by someone experienced with those fabrics and may be best done by the boat's original builder.

SOLID FRP LAMINATES

A small hole or break in a solid FRP laminate in which the damaged area is accessible from both sides is the easiest repair situation. You have a choice of whether to effect the repair from the inside or the outside. The advantage of making the repair from the inside is the ease of fairing the repair into the original hull surface.

In any case, the damaged area of the laminate is removed completely, usually by cutting it out with a saber saw. Blades intended for sawing metals and reinforced plastics are recommended. Cutting an FRP laminate is very tough going and blades wear out quickly. Before cutting the hole, however, it is important to survey the damage from inside the boat if possible, even if it means removing some furniture and equipment. Frequently the damaged area is larger than is obvious from the outside. For example, a small point impact on the exterior may result in a relatively and surprisingly large area of delamination that is visible only from the inside, where it is not hidden by pigmented gel coat. If the damage is not accessible from the inside, it may be possible to sound out the extent of delamination by tapping on the hull with a small wooden hammer. It is also possible to cut out increasingly large areas until a solid laminate is reached.

Once the damaged area has been cut away, the simplest repair involves beveling the edge of the laminate around the hole (Fig. 24). According to generally accepted industry practice, a thin laminate of $3/16$ inch or less should be beveled at an 8:1 angle. So, for example, the beveled area in a laminate $1/8$ inch thick would extend 1 inch ($1/8$ x 8 = 1) out from the edge of the hole. In addition, if the laminate is less than $3/16$ inch thick, the patch should be built up 25 percent thicker than the original laminate, overlapping beyond the beveled area.

The bevel angle for a laminate more than $3/16$ inch thick should be 16:1. This means, therefore, the beveled area for a $1/2$-inch-thick laminate would extend 8 inches ($1/2 \times 16 = 8$) back from the edge of the hole. The bevel angle is important to ensure an adequate area for the chemical bond between the original laminate and the patch. The integrity of the patch often depends entirely upon the strength of that bond. In any but a small patch, however, it is often desirable to install one or more stringers that extend beyond each side of the patch. The stringers not only help stiffen the repaired area, but also help tie the patch into the original laminate.

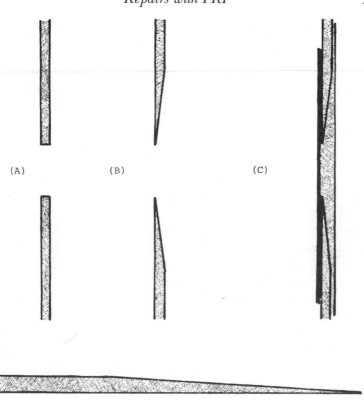

(A)   (B)   (C)

|—————— 4" ——————|

Fig. 24.   In repairing a small hole in a solid FRP panel, (a) the damaged area is cut out, (b) the edges of the hole are beveled, and (c) the patch is laid up against a backing plate taped or cemented to the panel. An FRP laminate ¼-inch thick (illustrated below the vertical panel) should be beveled back 4 inches from the edge of the hole, that is, a distance 16 times the thickness of the panel.

Earlier, it was noted that the advantage of effecting a repair from the inside is the greater ease of fairing the patch into the hull or deck surface. A 2-inch hole in a ½-inch laminate to fill in where a through-hull fitting has been removed, for example, will involve an area 2 inches in diameter on one side of the laminate and 18 inches in diameter (8-inch bevel plus 2-inch hole plus 8-inch bevel = 18) on the other side where the laminate has been beveled. Obviously, it is easier to make an "invisible" patch 2 inches in diameter than one 18 inches across.

In addition, when effecting a repair from the interior, a "mold" made of a piece of fiberboard, heavy cardboard, or other stiff backing covered with polyethylene film or Saran Wrap can be taped to the outside of the laminate. From that point on, you are laying up your patch in a female mold formed by the backing plate and the beveled edges of the hole. First, gel coat is brushed onto the area covered by the backing plate and allowed to cure. Next, a skin coat of one or two layers of 1.5-ounce mat (depending upon the thickness of the laminate) is applied and allowed to set up. And finally, alternating layers of mat and fiber glass boat cloth are applied. If the laminate is more than $3/16$ inch thick, the patch should be laid up in two or more stages to prevent excessive heat buildup as the laminate cures. In addition, each laminate should be progressively larger so that the patch "grows" with the beveled area.

If the repair is effected from the outside, it is necessary to provide some kind of a backing plate. If the area is accessible from the interior, the backing covered with polyethylene film or Saran Wrap can be taped to the inside. The plastic film will allow the backing plate to be removed when the patch has cured. If the area is not accessible from the interior, as when a hull liner or deck liner is in the way, contact cement can be used to hold the backing plate in place initially. The contact cement should be spread along the inner surface of the laminate around the edge of the opening and around the edge of the backing plate. No polyethylene or Saran Wrap is needed, since the backing plate for the patch will remain in place after the repair is completed. By putting a screw into the backing plate to serve as a handle, the backing plate can be positioned properly after it has been fit through the hole and pulled up against the inside of the laminate, mating the contact-cemented surfaces. Of course, the screw must then be removed. Such a backing will be sufficiently strong to apply the first layer of mat. After that initial mat layer has cured, subsequent laminations should be applied, ending with one or preferably two layers of mat.

When the lay-up is completed, the surface of the patch should be about 20 mils (less than $1/32$ inch) lower than the level of the gel coat of the original laminate to allow room for gel coat on the repaired area without creating a high spot. Before thickened gel coat is brushed onto the patch, however, the new FRP area should be carefully faired using sandpaper and, if necessary, a polyester or epoxy putty to fill in low spots. When the surface is properly faired, the edges of the repaired area should be taped (as in repairing a crack or gouge) and the gel coat applied to a level even with the top of the tape. When the gel coat has been spread evenly over the patch, it should either be covered with a film of Saran Wrap or polyethylene film or sprayed with polyvinyl alcohol (PVA) to provide the air barrier needed for the resin to cure. The film can be removed when the gel coat has cured. The PVA is readily washed off with water. Alternatively, though it is more difficult for an amateur to work with and thus not recommended, gel coat containing a wax surfacing agent may be used. In that case, it is not necessary to use PVA or a plastic film to seal the resin from the air. In applying gel coat containing a wax surfacing agent, however, it is important to avoid going back to brush out the gel coat once it has been applied, or the wax film that forms will be disturbed and the resin will not cure properly.

In working from the outside to repair a thin laminate requiring extra thickness in the patch, it will be necessary to sand away the gel coat for 2 or 3 inches beyond the beveled area, extending the extra laminates out over the sanded area, and then carefully fairing the edges of the patch into the original gel coat surface. However, each extra laminate should be larger than the one preceding it. In addition, the edges of each extra laminate should be faired into the existing surface before the next layer is applied. In this way, although the repaired area will be slightly higher than the original laminate, it will be hardly noticeable if the subsequent gel coat is blended well.

COMPOSITE CONSTRUCTION

The use of composite construction complicates the repair process somewhat. Two different circumstances tend to exist that cause need for repairs. One involves simple abrasion; the other involves impact. In the first, a boat may rub against a concrete dock edge, for example, and abrade through the outer FRP skin and into the core. Repairing that damage is relatively simple, assuming there is no water damage to the core. The edge of the outer skin around the damaged area is beveled as in working with a solid laminate, the damaged portion of the core built up using layers of mat and resin, the outer skin repaired using alternating layers of mat and woven fabric and the patch finished off as in working with a solid laminate. The same bevel angles apply, depending upon the thickness of the outer skin. If the core has been damaged by being wet, all wet core material must be removed and should be replaced using the same kind of core material. Repair to the outer FRP skin follows the procedure previously outlined.

In the second circumstance, in which damage has been caused by impact or a combination of impact and abrasion, close inspection is needed to determine whether the bond between the core and the inner skin has been damaged, particularly if there is otherwise no visible damage to the inner skin. This may require hiring a surveyor or other qualified expert to sound out the delaminated area from the inside as well as from the outside.

Once the extent of any delamination has been determined, the damaged area will need to be cut out. After the cutout has been completed, the edge of the hole should be examined carefully to be certain that damage does not extend beyond the cutout in any direction. If there is visible evidence of damage to the core material or of delamination between the core and either the inner or outer skin, the cutout should be enlarged.

If the damaged area is accessible from the inside, repairs are considerably easier than if all work must be done from outside the boat (Fig. 25). The inner skin can be beveled from the inside, the outer skin beveled from the outside, and each "skin" repaired separately. When the beveling has been completed, a section of core material—the same kind of core used to build the hull—is cut to fit snugly into the damaged area. The edges of the new piece of core material and of the core around the edges of the cutout should be coated with polyester putty that will harden to hold the new piece of core tightly in place once it has been positioned carefully in the hole.

This new section of core material will serve as a backing plate for both skins. The inner surface of the core should be coated with resin and a resin-rich laminate of 1.5-ounce mat applied. When that first mat layer has hardened, alternating layers of mat and woven fabric should be built up to repair the inner skin. After the inner skin has cured overnight, the outer surface of the core should be faired to ensure a smooth contour

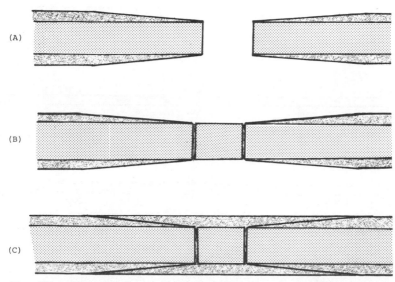

FIG. 25.   If a cored panel is accessible from both sides, the two skins can be beveled as shown in illustration (a). A new piece of core material is fit snugly into the hole (b) and "glued" to the surrounding core using resin or repair putty. The core then acts as a backing plate (c) for the repair patches for the two skins.

before laying up the FRP patch for the outer skin, again beginning by brushing resin onto the core and applying a resin-rich layer of 1.5-ounce mat.

If the damaged area cannot be reached from the interior of the boat, the repair is more difficult. After the damaged area has been cut away, you must (1) figure out how far the beveled area for the inner skin must extend out from the edge of the hole and (2) cut or grind away the outer skin and core to expose sufficient surface of the inner skin for the beveling (Fig. 26).

For example, if the inner skin is ¼ inch thick, the beveled area should be 4 inches wide around the hole. This means that the outer skin and the core must be removed for 4 inches around the edge of the hole, but with the inner skin remaining intact. Then the inner skin must be beveled, a backing plate installed as described for working with a solid FRP laminate, and alternating layers of mat and woven fabric laminated to form a patch

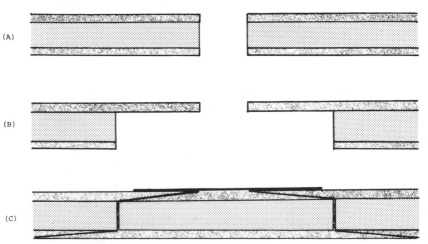

(A)

(B)

(C)

FIG. 26. When a cored panel is not accessible from both sides, the damaged area is cut away as in (a). Next a further cut is made in the outer skin and core removed as in (b) to expose the intact inner skin. The core should be removed for a large enough distance from the edge of the hole to allow proper beveling of the inner skin for patching. After the inner skin has been patched, the outer skin is beveled properly, a new section of core installed, and the repair completed (c) by patching the outer skin.

for the inner skin. If the inner skin is extremely thin, as it might be in a lightweight racer, the outer skin and core will have to be removed for an even greater distance to allow for overlap beyond the beveled area for the extra layers of reinforcing fabric needed to provide adequate strength to the inner skin patch. In this instance, a slightly thinner core than was used in the original construction may be required. At the least, the outer surface of the core will have to be sanded or ground down to compensate for the added thickness of the inner skin.

Once the edge of the outer skin has been beveled for the appropriate distance from the hole, a section of core material is cut to fit snugly in the area being repaired. Before installing the core, however, a resin-rich layer of 1.5-ounce mat is laminated to the exposed surface of the inner skin, resin brushed on what will be the inner surface of the core, and the new piece of core material pressed firmly in the hole against the still soft layer of mat. When the bond between the core and the inner skin has had ample opportunity to cure, 2 or more hours, the core surface should be faired and the repair to the outer skin completed.

MAKING LARGE REPAIRS

Large repairs are best made by experts. The boat will have to be cradled carefully to prevent the hull from becoming distorted when the damaged portions have been cut away. In addition, large repairs to the hull often are made most easily working from the interior of the boat to lay up the patch in a female mold placed against the outside of the hull. This may require major surgery to the interior accommodations. Although tearing out portions of the interior accommodations only to rebuild them later may seem extreme, the opportunity to use a female mold to lay up a new laminate to replace the damaged section of the hull makes any temporary disturbance to the interior worthwhile. It also makes it easier to install added reinforcement, such as stringers and other frames to strengthen the repaired area. The edge of the laminate where the damaged portion has been cut out should be beveled on the inner surface to receive the new lay-up before the mold has been set in place to avoid possible damage to the mold surface during the grinding operation.

There are essentially two ways to obtain a mold. One is to purchase one from the company that built your boat; the other is to build one for yourself. Assuming your boat is still in production, the manufacturer usually is willing to to make a mold for the damaged area of your boat. Most likely, however, the cost will be more than if you were to do the job yourself.

Unless you have a custom boat, the likelihood is that there is another boat just like yours somewhere nearby. If so, and if you are not in a hurry and are willing to ask, it may be possible to negotiate permission to make a mold for your boat from that sister ship. It will mean taking the sister ship out of service for at least 2 weeks, depending upon the size of the job, and it may involve removing some bottom paint and later repainting the bottom, but the opportunity to use that boat as a plug for your mold makes it all worthwhile. Alternatively, if the damaged section of your boat has not yet been cut away and still retains the original shape of the hull despite the damage, it may be possible, using plaster of Paris, to fill in the damaged area and shape the plaster to the original contours of your hull. In this way, your own hull can be used as the plug for the mold.

To make the mold itself, the surface of the plug is cleaned thoroughly. All dings, scratches, and other surface blemishes are repaired, and the area surrounding the section of interest is taped off and covered to protect the other surfaces. If plaster of Paris has been used to fill in the damaged area, it should be coated with several applications of lacquer. After a release agent has been applied to the plug, the mold-making process is started: Gel coat is applied and allowed to harden; three layers of 1.5-ounce mat are applied; and several stringers are taped into place to stiffen the panel. If the area is large, additional layers of mat may be needed. The stringers can be formed using hat sections of foam or by cutting the cardboard cores for rolls of paper towel in half lengthwise and taping them end to end across the panel using a 6-inch-wide strip of mat. As the strips of mat cure, it is important to watch for signs of the mold being distorted as the resin shrinks in curing. If such distortion occurs, the next time the stringers should be applied in shorter sections, with each section allowed to cure before the next is added.

When the mold has cured completely—a week if the person whose boat you are using as the plug gives you enough time—it is removed from the plug and any surface blemishes repaired. The surfacing agent should be removed from the boat used as the plug and, as a minimum, the boat's overall exterior finish restored to its previous good condition.

If another boat is not available, and if a mold is not available from the builder, it is usually possible to make a mold from your own boat as long as it is not damaged in the same area on both sides. Hal Roth accomplished this by shaping a series of wood frames to fit precisely down the good side of *Whisper's* hull, then turning the pieces 180 degrees on their verticle axes, and placing them in correct position over the hole in the other side of the hull (Fig. 27). These pieces were fastened together firmly in a lattice structure and a thin sheet of pressed fiberboard fit to the curve formed by the frames to make the mold surface. It should be noted, however, that if the hull surface being repaired forms a compound curve, it may be necessary to use several smaller pieces of fiberboard or thin plywood to form the mold surface.

Once a mold has been obtained—or made—it is put securely in position, prepared with a surfacing agent, and the lay-up begun. First, gel coat pigmented to match as closely as possible the original gel coat color is applied to the mold surface, using care to get gel coat all the way to the edge of hole. Next, two layers of 1.5-ounce mat are applied, the first with a slight excess of resin. Each layer of fabric, of course, is made progressively larger to accommodate the beveled edge of the hole.

If a solid laminate is used, the buildup would continue to a thickness of about $3/16$ of an inch and then be continued the next day. However, before resuming the lay-up, the laminate should be wiped down thoroughly with a solvent to clean the surface.

If the laminate contains a core, the procedures are identical to those described for repairing a smaller area, except that it will be the inner skin that is removed along with the core to allow room to bevel the outer skin properly. In any case, when the laminate is completed and fully cured, the mold is removed. If the mold had a good surface, the only fairing needed will be at the edges of the repair area. Most likely it will be necessary to paint the boat, but that is a small price to pay for having your boat back in good form.

Not all large repairs, of course, need such an elaborate mold. Damage to the stem or stern, for example, or to the deck or cabin house may be repaired more easily from the exterior using what is, in essence, a male mold consisting of plywood or pressed board placed behind or underneath the area to be repaired. When repairing the hull and deck along the shear of my for-

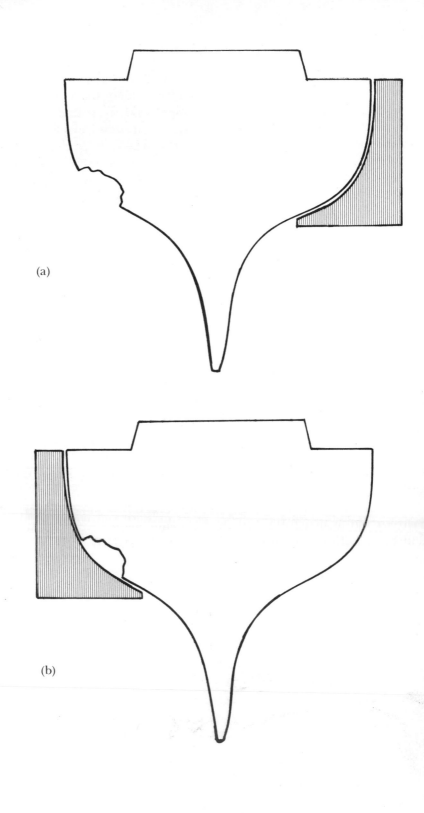

mer boat, for example, the yard bent a 1- by 2-inch piece of
mahogany to form the curve formerly made by the joint between
the hull and deck. They then erected a set of backing plates
that ran from the mahogany board to the good part of the deck
and from the board down to the good part of the hull. The
curved board and the backing plates served essentially as a male
mold and the patch was laminated over that rough mold, which,
except for the piece of mahogany, was removed later. In this
instance, of course, more work was needed to achieve a fair
surface finish than if a female mold had been used.

REPAIRS INVOLVING HULL LINERS, STRINGERS, AND BULKHEADS

Whenever the damaged area involves any interior reinforcement, the repair job is more complicated and it is not really
possible in the scope of this book to describe the variety of circumstances that can arise. However, certain generalizations are
worthwhile.

Hull Liners

Unless you are prepared to cut out and later rebuild a section
of a hull liner, you are forced to effect the repair from the
outside. This means you cannot use a mold to obtain a perfect
match of the former hull shape. However, the liner itself can
be used as the basis of a male mold for rebuilding the hull. For
example, after the damaged portion of the hull has been cut

Fig. 27.   (a) The correct hull line can be cut into sections of wood on the undamaged side of the hull to construct a framework for a mold of the damaged area. (b)
The plywood sections then are merely rotated 180
degrees around their vertical axes and they will fit around
the damaged side of the hull, showing clearly what the
hull line should be where the hull has been worn or cut
away.

out, a closed-cell polyurethane foam can be sprayed onto the liner to fill in what otherwise would be a space between the liner and the hull. Once that foam has hardened, it can be sanded to the shape of the hull. Using frames like those that Hal Roth used to make the mold for his boat to show where the outer surface of the hull will be, the foam can be faired to allow a space the thickness of the desired laminate between the foam and the wood framework. After the edges of the hull laminate have been beveled properly, the FRP patch is simply laminated against the foam, using a resin-rich layer of mat for the first laminate. Thereafter the process is identical to that used when building a custom hull using a foam core on a male mold (see Chapter 5).

Stringers

The presence of stringers in a damaged area may present two problems. The stringers may be cracked or broken, and the access may be difficult. The first problem is relatively simple to deal with conceptually. The second may present very real practical difficulties. However, any broken stringer or other frame reinforcement must be repaired to ensure structural integrity of the hull. In most instances, it would be preferable to effect the repair from inside the boat.

If a stringer is broken, it normally is repaired in much the same way a broken rib or stringer in wooden boat construction is repaired. A sister stringer is installed right alongside the broken area and fastened in place both with mechanical fasteners (stainless steel self-tapping screws or possibly bolts) and then covered with an FRP laminate. Depending upon the construction, it may be covered with several laminates.

Even if the stringer is not damaged, it will be necessary to cut and/or grind away the FRP layers used to bond it to the hull in the area that has been damaged. Later, when the hull damage has been repaired, a new fillet bond from the stringer to the hull will be needed. In addition, if the hull damage is being repaired from the outside, the exposed bottom of the stringer should be sanded clean and coated with resin to ensure a good bond between the bottom of the stringer itself and the new hull laminate. If the repair is being effected from the inside and the hull panel under the stringer is being replaced, the stringer should be cut out and then replaced after the hull repair has been made. If the stringer cannot be cut out completely, enough should be cut away from the bottom to allow adequate room to lay up the hull patch beneath the stringer. That cutout can be filled in later using foam, wood, and a heavy FRP fillet bond.

Bulkheads

Any damage to a structural bulkhead must be corrected before any repairs to an FRP boat are complete. When making such repairs, it is critically important to guard against hull distortion when removing structural bulkheads. In some instances, the job can be accomplished by cutting out the damaged section and replacing it with a new section of plywood; in others, the entire bulkhead may need replacing. In either case, although both a new section of bulkhead or the new bulkhead should be made to fit properly before the hull is repaired, it should not be set in place until after the hull lay-up has been completed. Then the bulkhead piece can be put in position, a trapezoidal section of foam cut to fit between the hull and the bulkhead to provide a nice radius for the laminates that will bond it in place, and the new fillet bond applied on both sides of the repaired bulkhead, extending at least 6 inches out onto the bulkhead and 4 to 6 inches or more onto the hull, as described in Chapter 6.

As in the case of stringers, even if the bulkhead itself is not damaged, the old fillet bonds should be cut away. The FRP laminate from the fillet bond that is remaining on the bulkhead also should be ground away to obtain a bare wood surface. The reason for this is that the impact that caused the hull damage may have broken the bond between the FRP laminate and the bulkhead itself. Left that way, a hard spot could develop in the hull. Removing the FRP laminate from the bulkhead also lets you be certain the impact did not cause any delamination of the plywood under the bond. Finally, you can be certain when you making major repairs yourself and letting an expert do the job for you.

It was noted earlier that major repairs probably should be done by experts. It is a truism to say that usually it is much more difficult to rebuild an existing structure than it would be to build it from scratch. The reason, of course, is that in building something from scratch, each piece goes into place in a logical order. In rebuilding that same item, each piece goes into place however you can get it there, because your effort to save as much of the original structure as possible gets in the way of "logical order." There is a difference, of course, between rebuilding a boat and repairing it. In the case of major repairs, however, the difference may be quite small, particularly as regards the requirements for the boat-building skills.

Moreover, the importance of doing the repair properly is more than cosmetic: Any major repair that is not done properly will compromise the integrity of the boat and, therefore, the safety of her crew and passengers. For this reason, although it is well to know basically what can be done to repair an FRP boat, what is involved in making that repair, and how the work should be done to effect the repair properly, discretion should be the better part of valor if you ever have a choice between making major repairs yourself and letting an expert do the job for you.

12

A Look Ahead
A Continuing Revolution
in the Works

The successful introduction of a budding fiber glass technology to the boating industry during the 1950s marked the beginning of the end of much boat building as an art. In place of the skilled craftsmen who shaped ribs and carefully fit planks to the graceful but complex curves of a hull came the relatively unskilled laborers of the glass shop. And in place of the hand-crafted, quasicustom wooden boat came the now familiar production line fiber glass boat. Today still more change is emerging as boat construction—no longer an art, but still in transition—moves closer to science.

There are several driving forces. At the top end of the market, where cost is not a major concern, the goal is often simply better performance, that is, more speed. In the rest of the market where cost *is* a major concern, improved performance may also be a factor, but usually for more complex reasons. Sailboat builders, for example, face a growing need to provide improved performance, because the notion that cruising boats must be slow boats incapable of moving upwind efficiently has finally been laid to rest. As a result, even sailors uninterested in racing are demanding "modern boat performance." There is also new rigging technology being developed for sailboats, a technology that has been initially popularized principally by the efforts of

Gary Hoyt on behalf of his Freedom yachts and their freestanding (unstayed) masts, one which some skeptics believe will prove only a fad, but one that others believe may evolve into a new generation of strong, lightweight spars made of carbon fiber-reinforced plastics rather than the extruded aluminum used almost universally in the United States today.

Builders also are feeling pressure for change as a result of the nation's shift to smaller automobiles and pickup trucks. The days of relatively inexpensive V-8 engines are numbered. As Detroit continues downsizing automobiles in the quest for better fuel economy, the production of V-8's is dwindling to the point at which some builders are concerned that V-8 engine blocks soon will no longer be produced in large enough numbers to make them available to the marine industry at a price most consumers are willing to pay. This means the powerboat industry is faced with the challenge of making tomorrow's boats move over the water at today's speeds without the benefit of today's large engines.

There is another fallout coming from the shift to smaller cars as well. Today's smaller cars and trucks cannot tow trailers carrying many of today's heavy boats. As a result, builders of trailerable boats are starting to look toward advanced technology to help them adapt to a new market need for boats that weigh less but provide the same range of size and accommodations the trailer-boating public has come to expect.

Other forces for change are coming from different directions. For example, boat building has become big business. With bigness has come increased attention to profitability, as yard managers must now answer to a corporate management more concerned about earnings statements than about tradition. Moreover, competition has stiffened significantly, not only among U.S. builders, but also between the U.S. industry and its overseas counterparts. The sailboat industry and the trawler segment of the powerboat industry have been particularly hard hit by imports from the Far East, where such advantages as low wage rates, relatively little government regulation, and low-cost materials enable builders to produce yachts for a price that U.S. builders simply cannot compete with on a cost basis alone—with present technology.

The combined effect of all of these forces is rapid change across a broad technological front. At one end is an increased emphasis on materials and engineering. In the middle, there is renewed emphasis on direct testing through development of experimental boats and new application of indirect testing methods using computerized design and stress analysis. At the other end, there are efforts to develop new production technology, efforts that run the gamut from applying computer controls to some segments of the production line to developing vacuum-assisted injection molding techniques to replace the wet lay-up technology now standard across the industry. The goal of all of these efforts is to build better boats with more efficient use of both materials and labor.

REINFORCING MATERIALS

Fabric Development

In years past, when a builder wanted extra strength in one area of the boat, he simply added a laminate of woven roving and mat throughout the hull. Today most builders limit the extra laminate to the general area in which it is needed. Tomorrow builders will be using new reinforcing fabrics to put extra strength precisely where it is needed. The fabrics that will make this kind of precision structural engineering possible in FRP boat construction are the new unidirectional rovings developed initially for aerospace applications but now finding their way into the boating industry. As noted in Chapter 2, single fabrics consisting of two and three layers of unidirectional rovings are now available. A bidirectional fabric stitched by a knitting process to chopped strand mat is also now in use, providing the same kind of convenience for nonwoven fabrics that Fabmat has provided for woven rovings.

The development of these unidirectional, bidirectional, and triaxial rovings has been hailed by many as the biggest breakthrough in reinforcing fibers for the boating industry. The reason is that they let the builder put the reinforcement where it is needed, and only there. These new materials are nonwoven fabrics of long, continuous filament glass fibers. As explained in Chapter 2, the fibers in each layer are generally oriented in a direction different from those in the layer below. The use of these new fabrics overcomes three inherent shortcomings of woven roving: (1) Woven fibers can shear each other under stress because the rovings run over and under each other; (2) woven fabrics have relatively little strength along the diagonal; and (3) about 55 percent of the reinforcing fibers in woven roving run along the length of the fabric, and 45 percent along the width of the fabric—always, whether or not that is where the reinforcement strength is needed.

Such factors have practical implications for boat builders. For example, tests by one builder suggest that use of the new triaxial fabric results in a laminate 30 percent stronger than one of the same weight made with woven roving. This means, of course, that builders can use triaxial fabric to build stronger boats of the same weight or lighter boats of the same stregth compared to boats they are building today using conventional woven reinforcement. Other tests suggest that the load strength of triaxial laminates is 40 percent more consistent from one lay-up to another than the load strength of laminates using woven rovings. This difference also offers opportunity to save weight. By reducing uncertainty in laminate performance, use of triaxial roving lets builders design more closely to the structural requirements of the boat rather than rely upon large safety factors to compensate for large uncertainties.

There are other differences as well. The uneven surface of woven roving has generally required use of chopped strand mat between layers of the woven fabric to ensure a good bond between layers of the laminate. With the high standards of quality control often possible in custom boatyards, the smooth surface of unidirectional fabrics lets builders save weight by omitting the mat between layers of roving.

The use of these new fabrics is not yet widespread. They are relatively expensive. Moreover, builders cannot simply substitute one of the new fabrics for woven roving and expect to accomplish anything except increased costs. The boat lay-up must be engineered specifically for the reinforcement used. But their time is coming. Custom yards already are using these fabrics for high-performance boats. A few of the more technologically advanced production boat builders are using the new fabrics in some of their new boats. Builders of smaller racing sailboats are also using these fabrics. Vanguard, Inc., for example, has been using triaxial roving in combination with other reinforcing materials to build its Finn class boats for well over a year and, at this writing, expects to use triaxial fabrics when it builds all of the Finns for the 1984 Olympics. How much does all of this add up to? Proform, Inc., one producer of these specialized fabrics, estimates triaxial roving will capture 10 percent of the market from woven roving in 5 years.

Epoxy Prepregs

Some builders also are looking beyond reinforcing materials on the one hand and plastic resins on the other to fully integrated systems of resin and reinforcement. And, when their eyes focus on the future, they are looking at epoxy prepregs. The reason for this is that the strength and weight of a laminate depend not only on the structure, form, and surface characteristics of the reinforcing fibers, but also upon both the structure of the resin and the quality of its marriage to the fibers. This resin matrix can be much more closely controlled when resin is applied to reinforcing fabric in the closely controlled conditions of a chemical process plant than in the laminating shed of a Florida, California, or Rhode Island boat builder. The resin-to-glass ratio can also be controlled more closely.

The complication of prepregs, of course, is the need for a vacuum bag system to compress the layers of the laminate structure into an integral unit and an oven to cure the laminate. The dividend, however, particularly when prepregs are used in conjunction with a core material—usually a honeycomb core— is greatly increased strength for less weight. As a rule of thumb, fiber glass prepregs used with honeycomb core will save 30 to 50 percent in the weight of a given laminate; with the use of Kevlar prepregs and honeycomb, weight savings is 60 percent.

There are multiple attractions to this kind of weight savings. Prepreg/honeycomb sheets already are used by some builders for lightweight structural bulkheads. Usually the bulkheads are molded under contract by a company that already has facilities to handle prepregs and honeycomb core. At least one large-boat builder, however, has installed an oven to test the potential for prepreg/honeycomb sandwich structures to replace heavy engine hatches that now require two strong men to open. Another builder is looking at a prepreg/honeycomb sandwich as one way to build an inboard/outboard powerboat that can be trailered behind today's small cars. Still another is testing a prepreg / honeycomb sandwich as the strong, lightweight hull and deck that will let him produce today's high-performance boats using tomorrow's low-performance engines from Detroit.

Prepregs have another factor going for them as well. As noted earlier, there is widespread concern within the boating industry that it will be faced with regulations limiting exposure to chemicals—particularly styrene—in the workplace. Styrene, of course, is a critical component of polyester resins, and resin makers already are developing formulations containing surfacing agents that help keep styrene from evaporating out of the resin. Epoxy resins however, do not contain styrene. Moreover, epoxy prepregs go into the mold dry in an air-conditioned room; there is little employee exposure to catalysts or other chemicals frequently associated with the use of polyester resins in a wet layup.

There is still one other growing attraction to the use of prepregs. As engineering becomes more important in boat design and construction, the use of prepregs offers builders additional opportunity to control the lay-up of their hull and deck more precisely by greatly simplifying the job of putting reinforcement right where the engineer wants it. There is no mess to encourage sloppiness, no rush to get the reinforcement laid out, sprayed, rolled, and squeegeed before the resin kicks. Instead, there is almost a clean room atmosphere and opportunity for a deliberate pace.

Core Materials

The trend to increased use of core materials in boat hulls as well as their decks already is well underway. Another trend is also developing: the use of core materials to save weight in building cabin soles, sun decks, and bulkheads. Moreover, the engineering involved is reaching beyond the comparatively simple insertion of a core between the inner and outer skins of a hull or deck. One example is the motor yacht hardtop mentioned earlier that is made using Klegecell foam core and carbon fiber reinforcement in the laminate. Another example from the same builder involves a 15- by 11-foot cabin sole in the main salon of one of his boats. The sole is supported only along its edges, leaving the entire bilge area below unobstructed. It is fabricated of a top surface of ¼-inch plywood, an FRP laminate of 1.5-ounce fiber glass mat, a 2-inch core of Klegecell foam, an FRP laminate of 1.5-ounce mat, and another layer of ¼-inch plywood. In essence, the inner and outer "skins" of this structure are composites of plywood and a single mat layer of fiber glass. Klegecell foam was chosen for the thick center "core" because it is the most lightweight conventional core material. This kind of engineering of internal structures is becoming more common, particularly in large boats, where cost is less of a constraint, in the quest to improve performance by engineering out unnecessary weight. It will spread to smaller boats, particularly to smaller powerboats, as the need to adapt to smaller engines and smaller towing vehicles make weight reduction a necessity rather than a luxury in that highly competitive market.

ENGINEERING

Over the centuries, boat engineering has been largely an empirical process. The builder constructed his boat based on the experience he and his predecessors had accumulated. If a problem arose in one boat, adjustments were made in the next. Today most boat building has not changed much. There are, however, breaths of change—change spurred in part by vendors trying to persuade builders to use their materials and systems, change spurred also by the incredible developments in computer technology since the late 1970s.

For example, in 1982 and 1983, Wellcraft had three test boats scheduled for construction to look at new materials. The first, a 26-foot runabout designed for speeds above 75 miles per hour, was constructed principally of Nomex honeycomb and Kevlar prepregs.

According to Wellcraft, the boat—named the Aramid Arrow—clearly demonstrated the performance advantages of the prepreg/honeycomb system. Eleven hundred pounds were cut out of the boat. The cost of that weight savings, however, was high. The process added $20,000 to the cost of a $35,000 boat, in large part because of the need to finish the exterior surface of the hull and deck by hand. As noted ealier in discussing custom hulls, such hand finishing is extremely labor intensive. Wellcraft says the challenge now is for the suppliers to develop materials and/or systems to bring production costs for prepreg/honeycomb construction down closer to those of more conventional FRP lay-ups.

Early in 1983, Wellcraft was planning to build both a 34-foot semidisplacement cruiser and a 38-foot high-performance speed boat to test a system using a polyurethane board stock core and a bidirectional roving in which 90 percent of the fibers run the length of the fabric and the remaining 10 percent are woven across the fabric. Projections made by the British company supplying the new materials suggested Wellcraft would save about 2,000 pounds on the 38-foot speed boat and 2,500 pounds on the 34-foot cruiser by using the new system. As noted earlier, polyurethane foam has not been widely used by the U.S. boating industry as a core material because of its tendency to crumble. The performance of this new core material, therefore, is one area Wellcraft will be watching closely.

At the other end of the spectrum, Hatteras Yachts is developing a computer system to accomplish some of the same kind of testing Wellcraft is doing, but before the first boat is built. The system is called "finite element analysis." It is a highly sophisticated mathematical technique developed for the aerospace industry to analyze the structural adequacy of a surface under different conditions. One of the first such computer programs was developed by the National Aeronautics and Space Administration.

In essence, finite element analysis lets an engineer save weight in his hull by helping him design more closely for the forces the boat will encounter. For example, the average impact load on the bottom of a 60-foot convertible planing across the waves is about 18 pounds per square inch (well over 1 ton per square foot). In some local sections of the hull, however, the pressures may be as much as 40 pounds per square inch (almost 3 tons per square foot). To withstand these loads, designers customarily have put large safety factors into their construction specifications. Finite element analysis lets the engineer use much smaller safety factors, because he knows just how strong the hull must be at virtually every point along the surface.

As with any such system, the engineer must begin with a certain amount of basic information. In this case, he starts by developing a hull design and deciding upon the construction method, the materials, and the lay-up schedule he wants to use. Once the hull lines are fed into the system, the computer breaks the hull surface into a grid, a network of small squares. The designer then must tell the computer such information as the loads on each square (forces of water buoyancy, wave impact, engine mounts, etc.), the shape or "geometry" of each square, and the physical strength properties of the hull in each square. These physical properties are derived from the list of materials, construction method, lay-up schedule, and such construction details as the distance of each grid square from a stringer or frame. Once the computer has all of this information, it can tell the engineer how that hull will react to the various loads the boat will encounter, showing him stress contours and the deflection of various hull sections. With this information, the designer can determine where additional reinforcement is needed as well as where excess can be removed. Moreover, the computer will show him what effect changes in the lamination schedule or design of stringer systems, and so on, have on the hull's performance as he fine-tunes the engineering detail (Photo 25).

Of course, all such computer analyses are only as good as the information put into them. Much of the information needed about dynamic loads on a boat in the water has been developed in tests conducted over the years by the U.S. Navy. Most of the physical property testing on fiber glass materials was done many years ago, however, and has not been adequately updated since, despite the fact that the resins and reinforcing fabrics have been improved enormously. For this reason, Hatteras Yachts has been developing its own materials laboratory and staff to test the physical properties of both conventional materials and the many newer materials now used for boat construction.

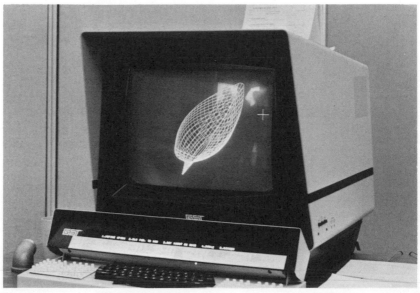

25. Computers like the one attached to this display terminal in the design engineering section of Hatteras Yachts are being used increasingly to work out the engineering details of modern motor yachts and sailboats. (Photo by Susan Roberts)

Another builder, Gulfstar, also is working to update results of the U.S. Navy tests—or, possibly, to make certain those test results apply to small craft. Gulfstar has put a series of transducers and a $50,000+ computer in one of its 60-foot boats sailing in the Southern Ocean Racing Circuit to measure the loads on various parts of that boat's hull as it encounters the full range of conditions found on that racing circuit. A similar system also was planned for one of their 48-foot motor yachts.

The use of computers in boat engineering, however, does not stop at finite element analysis or stress analysis. Increasingly, builders will be turning to computers to produce the working drawings used to build a boat. Traditionally, the industry has worked with prototypes, the first boat off the production line. In essence, the function of the prototype is to see how everything fits. The bugs then get worked out on the next few boats in the series.

The engineers at Hatteras believe computers can do away with production line prototypes, for computer technology now within the reach of boat builders lets engineers build their prototypes right in the computer. As a result, the engineering drawings are more accurate and parts made from them fit where they are supposed to go—the first time. The computer's advantage lies in its ability to work in three dimensions. On the drawing board, everything is flat. If a tank is designed at a drawing table and it is a few inches too deep, no one will know it until it is time to put the first tank into the first boat. Using a computer, the engineer can fit his "tank" into the boat right on his display screen and determine whether the fit is right before he prints out the drawing. The example is not farfetched. One of the first times Hatteras used its computer to check the accuracy of some of its engineering drawings, the computer showed the tanks for one of their new boats would have to be pushed through the bottom to fit under the deck. It was not an uncommon kind of error, caused by the difficulty humans have in making measurements of a complex three-dimensional shape illustrated on a two-dimensional drawing board. In a conventional situation, the tank would have been built; it would have been found to be too big when someone tried to fit it into the prototype and then cut back to proper size. Hopefully, also, the drawings would have been corrected. Today, however, engineers can build the prototype right in the computer, testing all of the detail drawings by fitting them into the computerized prototype before the first "blueprints" are produced. As a result, Hatteras believes it is now possible for the first boat in a new series to go through the production line smoothly without trial and error.

FRP SPARS FOR SAILBOATS

The idea of using fiber-reinforced plastic laminations to construct sailboat masts and booms is not new. Some of the first 40-foot Bounty sloops built in 1956 had fiber glass spars, and more than one designer has flirted with unstayed rigs—cat ketches—using FRP masts. However, FRP masts were either too flexible or, if the wall section of the mast was made thick enough to provide the needed stiffness, too heavy.

Today the use of carbon fiber reinforcement and epoxy resins to build strong, lightweight laminates is arousing new interest in the potential for advanced FRP technlogy to revolutionize the building of sailboat spars. The technology is exacting; the materials are costly; but more and more people are becoming believers. Nowhere in the boating industry is the marriage of engineering and computer science, advanced fiber reinforcement technology, and the use of epoxy prepregs further advanced than in the development of freestanding masts made of carbon fiber reinforcing fabrics and epoxy resins.

The leading producer of carbon fiber/epoxy resin spars in the United States is the Tillotson-Pearson yard in Warren, Rhode Island. In late 1982, Tillotson-Pearson reached agreement with Kenyon, the largest U.S. sparmaker, for Kenyon to market the carbon fiber spars. That agreement promised to accelerate use of the carbon fiber masts by the U.S. sailboat industry. It is unlikely, however, that many people will be retrofitting existing boats with unstayed carbon fiber masts. All of the heeling loads on the mast are borne by the mast partners (where the mast passes through the deck) and the mast step. Boats designed for unstayed rigs are constructed with major reinforcing in the deck around the mast partners to distribute the loads to the hull. Nor in the near term are stock carbon fiber masts that can be used in any of a number of boats likely to be produced; the costs of materials and production is too high.

The freestanding masts are specifically engineered for the stresses expected with each boat. A mast for a 20-foot boat, for example, designed for use with a spinnaker, must withstand the heavy point load the spinnaker places at the masthead. A mast designed to carry only a single sail attached along its full luff, in contrast, is designed for relatively even or diminishing loads along its length. The largest amount of reinforcement is in the lower portion of the mast, with diminishing amounts of the costly carbon fiber and epoxy resin required farther up the length of the spar. The masts are designed to withstand buckling, bending, and shear forces.

Initially, the carbon fiber masts were designed, constructed, and taken out for field trials with strain gauges placed at many locations along the mast to determine how the laminate design responded to the forces encountered. Today Tillotson-Pearson has built this field data into a computer program that makes such empirical testing unnecessary.

The masts are laid up over an aluminum mandrel, a male mold made to the shape and interior dimensions of the mast. Initially, a ribbon made up of thousands of continuous filament carbon fibers is wrapped spirally at a 45-degree angle up the length of the mandrel, with the edge of the ribbon butted against itself as it is wrapped. A second ribbon is wrapped spirally in the opposite direction. Next a layer of unidirectional carbon fiber roving is applied with the fibers running the length of the spar. The spirally wound reinforcing carries the buckling loads; the unidirectional roving running the length of the mast carries the bending loads. In the lower portion of the mast, the thickness of the laminate is increased to carry the twisting loads from the boom and the shear loads generated where the mast passes through the deck and at the mast step. There may be as few as 4 or, in the mast for the Freedom 65, for example, as many as 45 laminates of unidirectional roving in a mast. The number of spirally wound laminates is fewer. The carbon fiber fabrics are preimpregnated by Tillotson-Pearson with an epoxy resin to provide a 71 percent fiber-to-resin ratio. When the lay-up is completed, the mast is put into an oven and "baked" to effect a cure.

Although the suitability of the freestanding (unstayed) rig for broad application to pleasure boats is still subject to much discussion, the suitability of carbon fiber reinforcement and epoxy resins for construction of strong, lightweight masts and booms has been clearly demonstrated. Lady Pepperill, a modifed

Hunter 54 participating in the BOC Around-the-World single-handed race in 1982–1983 was equipped with two of the free-standing carbon fiber masts when she was rolled and pitch-poled in the Southern Ocean between Africa's Cape of Good Hope and Australia. Although the boat's hull suffered structural damage that resulted in her being abandoned, the two masts were still standing.

PRODUCTION TECHNOLOGY

Two separate trends appear most likely to affect the direction of production technology through the remainder of the 1980s. One is the introduction of computers to the production line; the other is a desire to reduce the labor content of FRP laminates and, at the same time, to increase control over the resin and fiber content of laminates. The first will affect mainly the construction of interior components; the second will affect construction of hulls and decks.

Computerized Production

Today a number of builders already use automated cutting tools to cut out pieces of plywood to size for interior components. This equipment, however, requires changing patterns for each different piece to be cut. It also requires positioning the plywood correctly in the machine. Computerization offers builders opportunity to streamline this operation significantly. In a fully computerized system, a worker could simply tell the computer the size and shape of the material placed on the cutting table, list the components to be cut from it, and then step back while the computerized cutting machine goes to work. Similar systems could be used for shaping teak trim, cutting veneers, and cutting smaller pieces used to assemble cabinets. In addition to saving time, such computerization may also reduce waste in materials because of the computer's ability to figure out how to cut the maximum number of finished components from each piece of lumber or sheet of plywood.

Laminating Technology

The increasing interest in prepregs as a system providing close control over resin and reinforcing fiber content of a laminate promises increasing use of vacuum bags and ovens in boat construction. As noted earlier, the only production boat builder using this technology at this writing is Force Engineering at Sarasota, Florida. Most of the work at Force involves use of epoxy prepregs with a honeycomb core. No gel coat is needed; the epoxy resin used in the prepreg material is an effective water barrier. Two-part polyurethane paints are used to shield the resin above the waterline from the sun's ultraviolet rays, as well as to provide an attractive finish. Bottom paint is applied directly over the epoxy laminate below the waterline.

The lay-up process itself provides a stark contrast to conditions in the laminating rooms used in conventional wet FRP lay-ups. After the mold is coated with a release agent, prepreg fabric covered on both sides with a protective film is removed from a refrigerated storeroom and, using patterns, cut to size and shape on a large worktable. The protective film is removed and the prepreg, which feels something like a slightly tacky oil cloth, is laid out in the mold. Along seams, the pieces of fabric are overlapped 3 inches. If a second prepreg layer is needed before the core is installed, it goes right over the first layer. Smaller pieces of material or strips of unidirectional roving in tape form can be used to provide extra reinforcement at high-stress points or to build up thickness for attaching fittings. Each piece of material is cut precisely to size and shape using patterns and placed precisely in the mold, ensuring uniformity of lay-up from one hull to the next. No mat is needed between layers, because the vacuum bag will compress each layer of fabric tightly against the other as the resin cures, providing a good interlayer bond. If it is necessary to keep an edge of the prepreg fabric from falling down, a heat gun resembling a small hair dryer is used to make the resin tacky.

Next the honeycomb core is cut, placed into the mold, and covered by an inner layer of prepreg material (Photo 26). When this lay-up has been completed, it is covered by a perforated film of Tedlar, whose function is to act as a release agent for

26. The use of prepregs provides a stark contrast in the work environment to a wet lay-up using a chopper gun. Using a hot-air gun resembling a hair dryer, workers tack precut pieces of reinforcing fabric
preimpregnated with epoxy resin into a deck mold, covering a honeycomb core (the dark strip). The hot air makes the epoxy resin tacky.
(Photo by Susan Roberts)

the layers to follow. The Tedlar film will not stick to the laminate, even after it has been cured. The final two layers consist
of an open-weave fabric resembling household window screen
and a disposable nylon film which is the "vacuum bag." The
function of the "window screen" is to hold the vacuum bag just
above the laminate to help achieve a good vacuum. The edge
of the vacuum bag is sealed along the edge of the mold using
an adhesive puttylike material.

At this point, the lay-up is ready for the vacuum pump and
oven. No resin has been sprayed, squeegeed, or rolled. Pieces

of fabric and honeycomb have simply been cut to size and placed neatly into the mold. When the vacuum is drawn, about 14 pounds of atmospheric pressure push against every square inch of the laminate, pressing it against the mold. It is like putting the lay-up in a press and applying about 1 ton of pressure (14 pounds per square inch are equal to 2,016 pounds per square foot) per square foot of laminate and then letting the resin cure. All air is removed from the lay-up, of course, and with the layers of fabric pressed hard against each other, there is little opportunity for voids in the laminate. With the vacuum drawn, the mold is placed in the oven and the temperature raised to an intermediate level that turns the resin to a semiliquid state. At this point, the resin flows to fill all bumps and valleys between the layers of fabric. It also climbs the walls of each cell (hole) in the honeycomb slightly, forming what looks like a miniature fillet bond along each cell wall and thereby bonding the core securely to the inner and outer skins. Except for formation of those pseudo-fillet bonds, the honeycomb cells themselves remain empty. After a preset dwell time, the oven temperature is increased to 250°F to effect the resin cure. The entire oven process takes about 4 to 6 hours. The hull or deck comes out of the oven with the cure completed, ready for installation of interior components. Before the boat is finished, however, the exterior surface must be prepared for painting. It is here that this process runs into difficulty because of the large amount of labor needed to achieve a good surface finish.

A technology newer to the boating industry, however, promises to compete with prepregs for the attention of builders in the late 1980s. That technology is injection molding, a system long used in the plastics industry for large-volume production of such small components as plastic through-hull fittings, toys, the tough plastic cases for many appliances, and plastic automotive parts. Conceptually, injection molding is simple. Resin is injected under pressure into a closed mold and allowed to cure. Sometimes, the resin may contain small reinforcing fibers a fraction of an inch long. When thousands of identical pieces are wanted, injection molding provides a fast, efficient means of production.

Until recently, however, there has been little effort to develop injection molding for use in boat building, where the system must accommodate the boat builder's need to use several layers of reinforcing fabric and, possibly, a core material. Today, however, technology is being developed that already is letting builders apply injection molding technology on a limited basis to FRP boat construction. One technique suitable for such relatively small moldings as hatch covers and battery boxes is called resin transfer molding. The other technique, already used successfully by Yamaha Motor Company in Japan to build several hundred 10-foot sailing dinghyes, involves a system of vacuum-assisted resin transfer molding. Both systems allow close control over the ratio of resin to reinforcing fiber, because only a measured amount of resin is injected into the mold—a sharp contrast to conventional wet lay-ups where an operator sprays resin into the open mold and must judge how much resin is needed by how the laminate looks.

In both the plain and vacuum-assisted resin transfer systems, the mold consists of female and male counterparts that fit one inside the other, leaving only a relatively narrow space between them. After the two mold halves have been prepared with a mold release agent, the reinforcing fabric is laid carefully into the female half of the mold. The male mold is then put into place, preparatory to injecting the resin. At this point, the two molding techniques take different paths.

In "plain" resin transfer molding, a series of plastic tubes are placed around the edge of the molds to allow air to escape from inside the mold as it is filled. Resin is then pumped into the mold until it begins to come out the plastic tubes. As each tube begins to fill with resin, it is closed off. Resin transfer molding already is being used at least experimentally by several builders, including Viking Yachts, which has been using it to mold cockpit hatches, swim platforms, and radar arches—even for freshwater tanks and wastewater holding tanks. Viking reports that resin transfer molding has reduced the production time for its radar arches by 90 percent. Plain resin transfer molding, however, probably is limited in application to relatively small components because of the difficulty in moving resin through a large mold filled with layers of reinforcing fabric by simply pushing (pumping) it into the mold.

Yamaha's experiments producing a 10-foot sailing dinghy using vacuum-assisted resin transfer molding, however, have demonstrated the feasibility of this system for production of larger components, including even larger hulls and decks. In a production run of 500 dinghyes, Yamaha engineers report that the vacuum-assisted resin transfer molding system yielded laminates with properties similar to those of a hand lay-up, but at a higher cost because of significantly higher mold costs. The vacuum-assisted resin transfer molding system, however, reduced the labor content of the dinghy by 30 percent. Among the keys to making the system more practical, particularly for larger boats, according to Yamaha, are reducing mold costs, learning more about the stiffness required for larger molds, and developing resins that will flow more easily through the mold, shrink less when curing, and give off less heat as they cure.

In the case of both prepregs and injection molding, of course, the key to any widespread use of these technologies will come down to the balance between cost and the demand for performance. Because of the costs involved in developing these systems, their use to build large boat hulls and decks probably will be reserved in the foreseeable future to the bold few who want to be on the cutting edge of their industry's technology.

At this writing, two such entrepreneurial groups, Ian Bruce in Canada in partnership with designer Bruce Farr in Annapolis, and Jeremy Rogers in England, were developing high-performance one-design sailboats in the 28- to 40-foot range using vacuum-assisted injection molding. A third, Dick Lazarra of Gulfstar, has constructed a 100-foot-long oven to build large powerboats and sailboats using prepreg/honeycomb technology under a new corporate structure, Lazarra Marine Corporation. Beyond such isolated endeavors, however, use of prepregs and injection molding technology are more likely to find most use in production of smaller components where, in the case of prepreg/honeycomb systems, weight savings make the cost worthwhile or, in the case of injection molding, mold costs are relatively low, labor savings relatively high, and the production relatively long.

Index